olive oil

olive oil

cooking, exploring, enjoying

clare ferguson
photography by peter cassidy

RYLAND
PETERS
& SMALL
LONDON NEW YORK

First published in Great Britain in 2000
This edition published in 2005
Ryland Peters & Small
20–21 Jockey's Fields
London WC1R 4BW
www.rylandpeters.com

10 9 8 7 6 5 4 3 2 1

ISBN 1 84172 872 1

A CIP catalogue record for this book is
available from the British Library.

Printed in China

Dedication

To my husband Ian Ferguson who,
25 years ago, took me to Greece,
where I first tasted superb extra virgin.

Notes

All spoon measurements are level unless
otherwise noted.

Ovens should be preheated to the specified
temperature. Recipes in this book were tested
with a fan-assisted oven. If using a regular oven,
increase the cooking times according to the
manufacturer's instructions.

Eggs are medium unless otherwise specified.
Uncooked or partly cooked eggs should not be
served to the very old, frail, young children,
pregnant women or those with compromised
immune systems.

Designer **Sarah Fraser**
Commissioning Editor
Elsa Petersen-Schepelern
Production **Gavin Bradshaw**
Picture Research **Tracy Ogino**
Art Director **Gabriella Le Grazie**
Publishing Director **Alison Starling**

Food Stylist **Clare Ferguson**
Assistant Food Stylist **Fiona Smith**
Prop Stylist **Helen Trent**
Index **Hilary Bird**

The hardback version of this book was published
under the title *Extra Virgin: Cooking with Olive Oil*.

contents

introduction

Each time we drive down the serpentine roads to our holiday *spitaiki* (tiny house) on Zakynthos, one of the Ionian Islands of Greece, the old joy comes soaring back. The land is as tough, tender and timeless as the olives, oleasters and thorn bushes rooted to the stony ground. Three old, bony olive trees, protective and patient, lean over our empty sheepfold as they have done for decades. Our neighbours press the olives in our absence during the winter. In the summer, if we are lucky, we will enjoy some of the deep, fruity, green-gold unfiltered oil on our bread within hours of our arrival.

This book celebrates extra virgin, the olive oil that can revolutionize our health and well-being, enliven our palates and warm our hearts. No wonder it has been prized for millennia.

Most plant oils are made from seeds. Almost all of these, to be economic, must be treated by chemical extraction and refining, extreme heat and pressure, solvents, bleaches, acids, alkalis and deodorizers, so that most volatile flavours are lost. However, cold-pressed olive oil (the one to look for) may be regarded as a wholly natural fruit juice, since it is mechanically extracted by simple squeezing. A bottle of really superb, estate-bottled, cold-pressed, extra virgin olive oil may cost more than the equivalent amount of champagne, since it takes about 5 kg of olives to make just 1 litre of this wonderful substance. But it is worth every penny.

Olive oil is a nutritional marvel as well as a gastronomic joy in that it also keeps its distinctive, complex flavour and aroma and stays chemically

intact, with built-in, health-giving nutrients such as tocopherol
(vitamin E) to keep it stable. Simply stated, it is one of the greatest,
most versatile foods ever known – and tastes utterly marvellous too. It
is excellent for general cooking, and even for deep-frying, since it
doesn't degrade, even during prolonged use at high temperatures.

For well over two millennia, olive trees, their fruit and their oil have
been integral to the religion, customs, culture and culinary traditions
of the Mediterranean.

Today, olive oil is one of the world's biggest health stories. Medical
discoveries confirmed in the late 1970s and early 80s that olive oil had
revolutionary properties. These were mainly linked to its high levels of
mono-unsaturated fatty acids which could guard against heart
disease. In addition, because of its anti-oxidant properties, it could
reduce free-radical damage in cells and therefore minimize the effects
of ageing and even protect against cancer. True, cold-pressed, extra
virgin contains useful polyphenols and there are more than 100 minor
components yet to be studied and evaluated.

making olive oil

In early autumn, the tiny, hard, pear-shaped olive fruits give no inkling of the richness to come. By late autumn and early winter, the olives are green, plump, succulent and perfect for making early-picked oil. Later the rosy, purplish, dark-brown fruits will yield quite a different oil.

In the cool climate of Northern Europe, people kept cows and so ate butter. In the south, families had their olive tree, its olives and its oil. Even if the tree was far off, on stony terrain, it needed little upkeep and, once established, it was a sure source of income.

Modern olive culture has changed all this. We know now that olive trees thrive best in correctly watered, rock-free, fertile soil on appropriate terrain. All over the world massive olive groves attest to this. Olive cultivation is still laborious and money-intensive, especially if you compare it with easily and cheaply extracted oils from a huge list of exploitable tropical seeds that can go into any number of formulations of so-called 'vegetable oils' – a particularly unhelpful term. Even worse, they are used to make the dreaded hydrogenated oil margarines, which are vegetable oils 'hardened' by hydrogenation: these lose the benefits of polyunsaturates and gain numerous disadvantages, including the problems posed by saturates.

Olive oil, thank goodness, can be made from the pressed juices of the olive and nothing else, by law. But the olive oil industry must evolve to compete, to be efficient, profitable and mass market. Scientists and agri-business advisers insist on the planting of huge groves of over 1,000 trees per hectare to justify 'remodelling' of terrain and the massive outlay on machinery. They urge abandoning the lovely terraced slopes created by generations of olive farmers unless systems with mechanical watering and harvesting gear can be designed to suit them.

Sadly, 'rationalization' means that many of the old groves, feral and uneconomical olive plantings have been all but deserted by the old olive growers who have quit the country for the cities. These groves may, alas, fade out. In Italy and France, where wages are high, this is particularly the case. Even in Spain and Portugal many old trees are being left to languish. However, prestigious regions such as Liguria, Tuscany, Sardinia and Provence still thrive. Spain and Greece continue to supply the market with large quantities of excellent extra virgin and virgin olive oils (some of which, however, is blended to some degree of uniformity, rather than individuality, for a mass market, competitive product). Increasingly, much production is being relocated to other Mediterranean sites such as Turkey and Tunisia where the wage demands are lower and harvest workers more readily available, as are grants from EU sources.

the harvest

Ideally, olives to be pressed for oil should be picked carefully from the trees by hand. But they are stubborn fruit and picking is not only tricky but physically tiring.

Fully ripe olives produce the most oil and are more profitable. However many believe the best oil is from green-ripe fruit since ripe olives damage more easily and can fall and bruise, sustaining enzyme and oxidation damage that affect taste.

Olives should be dropped gently into baskets, then into boxes. Any fruit that falls from the tree should be picked up quickly – daily if possible. The fruit must be clean and free of twigs and leaves before crushing. The fruit should go to the pressing house, be kept cool and processed without delay, within 12–36 hours. On small estates the fruit may be processed immediately, but this isn't easy at a large plant, when it is hot and there are many olives from many different sources waiting in line to be treated. They can become affected by the heat as they stand and this may compromise quality and flavour.

Harvesting work is seasonal – a few weeks to a couple of months of each year at most. Large-scale agri-business investors see this small-scale approach as archaic, charming, but impossible. In the past, olive growers could and did appreciate the keen demands and skill required but, since harvest took place in late autumn and winter, other agricultural tasks were minimal at these times and the system could somehow work.

Many Mediterranean sailors for example went to sea in summer, then stayed at home to nurture and harvest their olive terraces in winter. More recently, agricultural development grants in the European Union have become commonplace and people have abandoned the sea as a partial source of their livelihoods. Now they can tend their farms and olive groves full-time.

The small local harvests, apart from in agri-tourism areas, are becoming less common, whereas once it was a high point of the year. Typically, hard labour would be followed by great communal feasts, singing, ritual fun and jollity – an affirmation of the bounty of nature, a symbol of renewal.

extracting the oil

There are many alternatives for extracting the oil, as in cultivation and harvesting. Some are old, slow, demanding, small in scale, expensive in effort, but superb in result.

Others, used in large industrial plants, are centrifuging processes completed in a series of stages – superfast, so somewhat violent to the oil molecules. By such processes – economical, consistent and effortless – traditionalists feel that harm is done to the taste and chemical structure of the oil. Luckily there are some more intermediate methods, like the sinolea process, which involves spinning fine blades. There is yet another extraction method using a centrifuge operating at gentler speeds, a rapid process popular with some producers. Others prefer the old, classic vertical press with its mats and spindles, which gives fine oil without compromising flavour and chemical quality, as long as great care is taken with hygiene. These are less cost-effective because they require slower, more precise operation on a smallish scale, but are gaining new relevance in the resurgence of interest in boutique and artisanal products.

Finally there is filtering, tasting, blending, grading, bottling, labelling, packaging and transport to local and international markets.

Then, there it is on your kitchen shelf – a handsome bottle of extra virgin olive oil ready for use. This book is a celebration and exploration of some of the pleasures of cooking and eating enhanced by olive oil.

Unlike many fat or oil products which can be manufactured, olive oil can only come from olives. In addition, not all olive oil is extra virgin, the purest form. Only about ten per cent of the olive oil produced in the world is top class virgin oil (five different designated grades). The remainder is refined to remove flaws or impurities. Some of this refined olive oil will be blended with top-grade virgin oils to create a serviceable bulk product termed simply 'olive oil'. This tastes less good and is cheaper too, because it is more processed and is also less distinctive, but it is consistent and useful in its own right.

Try to learn and understand the basic technical terms that the international olive oil trade insists on as mandatory. Olive oils are graded on their amount of free acidity (which should be

small) and on their 'organoleptic' (smell and taste) qualities, determined by skilled grading experts. Today there are also precise chemical analyses such as gas/liquid chromatography that can detect any abuses (illegal or unacceptable substances in the olive oil). From time to time government authorities conduct random tests on olive oil samples taken from the shelves of stores. Such information can be found on (DEFRA), Britain's Department for Environment, Food and Rural Affairs website (www.defra.gov.uk), and reveal some surprising facts such as a small number of products that are not exactly of the quality their labels claim. Inform yourself: be sceptical.

As well as these official classifications, I have also listed other terms which may be present on the label. Many of these give precise descriptions, such as 'first, cold-pressed', 'estate bottled' or 'unfiltered', which the producer is proud to tell you: these are valuable in assessing quality and style. Other terms such as 'lite' or 'light' are not official terms so may be very misleading and unhelpful. Be vigilant. Like any well-produced food, the more there are specifics given, the more you can discover about quality. Look for relevant terms on the label, but be critical. Some can be irrelevant.

VIRGIN OLIVE OIL is any oil obtained solely from the olive by mechanical or other physical methods, under thermal conditions that do not cause any alteration of the oil. The only processes permitted are washing, extraction, decanting, centrifuging and filtering. Solvent use is not permitted.

'Virgin' olive oil is a technical term. It has five grades. In descending order of quality they are:

High standard (HS) olive oil A relatively new standard, indicating highest quality products. Its tests are even more stringent than those for extra virgin status: chemical, organoleptic, nutritional and health values are all taken into account.

Extra virgin olive oil Virgin oil of perfect aroma and flavour (high organoleptic quality) and with free acidity of no more than 1 per cent.

Note Many of these will be 'commercial' extra virgin olive oils, skilfully blended to a standard maintained from year to year, and to a price. They may come from different regions and countries. Others are single estate, often unblended, more expensive and very pronounced in flavour.

Virgin olive oil/fine olive oil Virgin oil with a perfect aroma or flavour and with allowable free acidity of up to 2 per cent.

Ordinary/semi-fine virgin olive oil Virgin oil of good but not perfect taste and aroma and with allowable free acidity levels of up to 3.3 per cent.

Lampante virgin olive oil (lamp oil) Poor-tasting and poor-smelling virgin oil with free acidity of more than 3.3 per cent. Unfit for human consumption in its original state, it should be refined to make it suitable as a foodstuff. Suitable for 'technical purposes' only, for example the textile or cosmetic industries.

THREE FURTHER GRADES SET BY THE INTERNATIONAL OLIVE OIL COUNCIL

Lower than virgin, these make up 90 per cent of world production, some as food, some for industrial use.

Refined olive oil Refined from virgin oils (usually lampantes) by processes which, by law, must not alter the oil's initial glyceride structure.

Olive oil/pure olive oil Specific foodstuff terms used on a label to mean a blend of refined olive and virgin olive oil, fit for human consumption. Some people use it for frying, others use it in general cooking where 'Mediterranean distinctiveness' is not required.

Olive-pomace oil Pomace is debris left over after extraction of virgin oils, treated with chemical solvents such as hexane, carbon sulphide or trichlorethylene. It excludes oils mixed with oils of other kinds (such as seed oils) and those obtained by re-esterification. Most discerning cooks avoid oil in this category.

THREE FURTHER CATEGORIES Crude olive-pomace oil, refined olive-pomace oil and olive-pomace oil. Heavily chemically

processed, these are 'bottom of the barrel'. They lack most qualities that made olive oil valuable in the first place: they are avoided by anyone who puts their palate ahead of their purse or cares about optimum health.

what's on the label

First, cold-pressed

Exactly what it says: the very first pressing, with little or no heat applied.
Often obtained using traditional methods and small scale production.
A superb product retaining its natural goodness and distinctiveness, but
often expensive.

Cold-pressed/'traditional manner pressing'

Simply extracted without any heat above 28°C (82°F), but perhaps from
the second pressing of the same olives. Still a good product, keeping
many healthy qualities and flavour.

Estate-bottled/single-estate oils

Top quality, premium-price, absolutely superb oils, that are often made
from hand-picked olives and cold-pressed within hours of picking.
Probably from a single family estate or farm, it may bear the family name
and logo. It is grown, extracted and packaged on home ground. The
important regions in the Americas, Australia, New Zealand and even
South Africa, as well as the great oil-producing areas of Europe, now
produce these oils.

Affiorato/flor de aceite/lágrima

Also known as 'flowers' or 'tears'. This is 'free run' oil – wonderful stuff, it
will often have been roughly crushed, probably between old millstones,
but not pressed: the oil merely runs off and is collected. This is rare and
very desirable.

In ancient Palestine, the finest of all oil was obtained simply by piling up
the ripe olives in a basket or dome-shaped space cut into a rock, with a
hole in the base. The gravity-driven run-off was collected and the oil
scooped off the top using a shell or a leaf. This process, called *à la
feuille*, still happens in some parts of the world – for example in Spain,
France, Greece, even New Zealand.

Date and year of pressing

This tells you the age of the oil – aim for oil as young as possible. Very new, young oil may have a particularly pungent bitterness, too strong for some palates, but it softens within several months. No oil lasts well for more than one year. Sometimes a bottling number is given as well – a process that implies artisanal care and quality.

Unfiltered

Means one less process: it implies excellent olive oil and careful handling. Often murky but delicious, it is described as 'veiled', since 'cloudy' would infer a fault. Many Spanish and French producers prefer it and some New World producers do too. Some like to use cotton wool in a sieve for a very light system of filtering. This will remove any unhelpful solids that might otherwise affect longevity.

Single varietals/blends

Sometimes only one variety of olive is used, sometimes a blend. This is up to the producer. Stylish blends are often excellent and single varietals can be too.

Designation of origin

Refers to specifics applied to olive oils from designated regions or zones that safeguard particular local traditions, olive types and/or characteristics. In Spain it is called DO, in Greece PGI or PPO, in Italy DOC.

Organic production/ecological production

Many small village oil producers and even some small co-operatives cultivate olives using age-old organic farming methods approved by certified agencies and monitored closely.

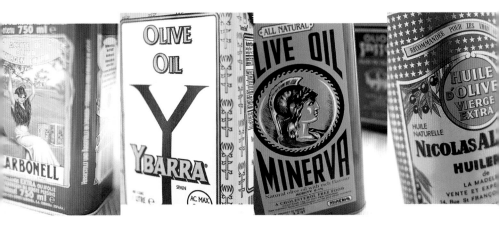

'Produce of' and 'packed in' labelling

Until EU rules recently outlawed it, 'produce of' could mean merely the last location at which the agricultural product was 'substantially altered in some way'. So Greek and Spanish oils bulk-exported and blended, if bottled in Italy, could legitimately but misleadingly claim to be 'produce of Italy'. Read the small print carefully.

Making your selection of olive oil

How to choose? Good suppliers, proud of their products, will usually organize a tasting, so go to a reputable merchant. But you should also select different oils, like wines, for their specific qualities. Keep your own cooking and eating needs, your taste preferences and your pocket in mind.

Choose an excellent, first cold-pressed or *affiorato* oil to trickle over foods at the table or to use with bread instead of butter.

Two other cold-pressed, extra virgin olive oils, one peppery, one mellow, can be used for salads, pasta, soups, on bread, in dressings and over seafood – pour it straight from the bottle.

Keep some less expensive, blended, mass-market grade, extra virgin olive oil for general cooking purposes including frying – this is a very versatile product. In frying, contrary to common belief, olive oil cooks hot, doesn't break down, keeps a protective crust around the food and is absorbed less than many other oils.

Select a virgin or ordinary virgin olive oil for mayonnaise and baking or just 'olive oil,' also called 'pure olive oil' (a blend of refined and virgin), for deep-frying or bulk baking. It will cost less, be blander.

Note Most good cooks steer well clear of low-grade oils. I don't use any olive oil other than extra virgin in the kitchen, but ours is a small household, not a giant extended family (in which case I might well use a more economical grade). Even so, I could never use any category of pomace: heavily processed, chemically stripped, cheap, commodity oils recycled from the detritus. Why not use a good-quality, cold-pressed seed oil instead, or mix ordinary virgin with extra virgin.

The Healthy Oil

Olive oil is one of the most delicious and natural of all lipids (fats) and an absolute health bonus. By choosing the lower grades you deprive yourself of some of the benefits. Even so, any olive oil still contains good levels of monounsaturates and increases helpful HDL (High Density Lipoprotein) levels while also reducing bad LDL (Low Density Lipoprotein) cholesterol levels in a way known to promote heart health. It is the natural anti-oxidant effects, helpful in combatting the harmful effects of free radicals, that are lost by using the more processed olive oils, and less chance, too of changes producing trans-fatty acids. Extra virgin olive oil contains 1.5–2 per cent phytonutrients such as vitamins, phenols and volatile taste components: part of its uniqueness.

northern and central italy

Olive trees are one of the most fundamentally characteristic aspects of the Italian landscape. Today, just as in the past, Italy's best, estate-bottled, extra virgin olive oils continue to astound and delight connoisseurs the world over. Grape vines, often side by side with olive trees, continue an age-old epicurean tradition.

From the sixth century BC, for many hundreds of years, olives changed the cultural, culinary and economic landscape of Italy and the wider Mediterranean area. The Etruscans, the pre-Roman inhabitants of Tuscany, used olive branches and leaves to decorate their burial chambers. Early Christians used them in their catacombs, and branches are still used on Palm Sunday. In Imperial Rome, citizens paid their taxes in olive oil, and sophisticated methods of storage were created for its export on ships specially modified for its safe and effective transport.

Today Italy is the most celebrated source of extra virgin olive oil and Tuscany and Umbria are uppermost in the mind as sources of green, grassy, characterful, often gutsy oils, sometimes with a peppery aftertaste and distinct, pungent, even bitter tang. Liguria in the north, the home of pesto, has its own, softer, more delicate style of oil – fresh, light and smooth, and much appreciated by Italians from all parts of Italy.

The traditional method of harvest is hand-picking – expensive in time and labour and, these days, practical only on old, traditional estates or by small growers. Old trees often dictate the traditional methods. Hand-picking involves stroking or combing with metal or plastic combs, or very skilled 'milking' of the fruit off the trees. But the type and size of fruit, its ripeness and resistance to plucking are all relevant. Picking a tree can take from

20 minutes to several hours, depending on the number of pickers, the tree's size, shape and age and the surrounding terrain. Pickers, holding ladders and baskets for others high up in a tree, may gossip or sing while they wait. Shaking the trees or knocking off the fruit into nets or cloths are less precise methods and may damage the trees. It can cause the olives to oxidize or even ferment. High-tech harvesting, on the other hand, may use, among other techniques, hydraulic vibrating machines – effective only in rationalized, replanted groves.

Italy is the world's second largest producer of olive oil, but it imports a great deal of bulk oils from, for example, Spain and Greece. These, in turn, may be blended to create products desirable for local use and also for its massive export market.

TENUTA DI VALGIAN
Olio
Extra Vergine
di Oliva

Messo in bottiglia nella
TENUTA DI VALGIANO
Valgiano Lucca Italia

500 ml   e   17 fl. oz.

Raccolto Nov

southern italy

Olive trees are Italy's grace, a significant part of her Mediterranean identity. It was the Ancient Greeks who originally introduced the olive tree to the Italians and it is in the Western Greek colonies of Southern Italy and Sicily, after all, where the best-preserved Greek ruins are to be found and some of the finest olive oil is produced.

Olives thrive in the valleys, on rocky heights and beside the windswept beaches of Sardinia. In Sicily, they are interspersed, silvery green and gold, with lemons and wheat. Olives alternate with vines, umbrella pines and cascades of flowers on the islands in the Gulf of Naples. They grow wild and straggly in the temples of Agrigento and thrive on the little volcanic islands off the north coast of Africa, from whence the olive probably traced its original route into Italy. In Positano, on the magnificent Amalfi Coast, olive and pine trees seem to tumble down the hillsides to the sea, sharing the soil with lush vegetables and scented flowers.

Southern Italian oils tend to be gorgeous, lightly fragrant, and perfect with local produce and herbs, in particular basil. Two typical oil styles from the south taste sweet, light and chocolaty, or mildly bitter with an almond tang and a scent of green leaves.

The six southern regions of Italy produce 80–90 per cent of Italy's oil. About half comes from Puglia, with Calabria, Sicily and Campania contributing the rest. These are the oils used in Italian kitchens as everyday oils.

Typical descriptions of oils can be misleading. The usual belief about southern oils is that they tend to be yellow, soft, mellow, less piquant than those of the north and even buttery in style. This is to some extent accurate

since late picking of black-ripe olives tends to be the norm here, while in Tuscany and Umbria where temperatures are cooler, picking is more likely to be from green-ripe olives. Because, too, of the mass production in the south, which is often done for big multinational companies, a more businesslike approach is expected. This often produces a correspondingly blander result, rather than the spicier flavours obtained from an artisan's approach. Certainly, some of the different production values, such as delays between picking and pressing, do tend to affect the final quality of some southern oils.

Other southern oils utterly defy this trend – estate-bottled oil from southern Sicily has a gold-green colour, a grassy, tomato-skin aroma, a distinct bitter green note followed by a full, fruit finish. It is superbly individual and there are many others in this class.

In Puglia, the aficionados often declare that some of the best olive oil has a faint but clear whiff of bitter almonds, perhaps borrowed from the almond trees which are grown among the olives – one can envisage the old trees entwining their roots under the soil and borrowing scent from each other.

HUILE D'OLIVE VIERGE EXTRA

FRUITS CHOISIS

1ère PRESSION À FROID

NICOLAS ALZIAR

HUILERIE

DE
LA MADELEINE

NICE

huile provenant CEE F 028

50 cl

MARQUE DE

FABRIQUE

south of france

Glorious Provence, unique in France for its time-worn olive groves, herb-scented hillsides and wild, romantic coastline, has been the inspiration for countless artists and writers, as well as chefs and grateful gourmands from all over the world. French extra virgin olive oils often echo the spirit of the terroir, with an elegant, aromatic freshness that is an absolute joy.

In international olive oil terms, France is a very small player, producing only 2,300 metric tonnes per year. Even so, its influence is huge. This is partly because the South of France has been a magnet for the 'great and the good' and a drawcard for many European and American expatriates who are fascinated by its food culture in general and its olive culture in particular.

However, in spite of changes in the rural economy and periodic frost-damage to the groves, there is now a rise in the desirability of olive oil as a valued and delicious healthy food and the decline has been somewhat arrested. Single-estate French oils are now considered some of the world's most superb. Even so, France cannot satisfy its own market, and so imports oil from other regions such as Sardinia and North Africa.

Related, happily, to good oil is a natural propensity of the French to gourmandize. The French have always prized fine food, fine wines and the culture of the table. Though butter has always had its epicurean role in northern French cuisine, olive oil along with lard, duck and goose fat have also had their valued roles in Provence and the South-west.

As in other Mediterranean regions, there is a dichotomy between the old and the new. Most French producers prefer the modern, continuous system of linked centrifuges to grind the pulp and spin out the oil. They are fast and easy to run. Growers of the old school prefer the traditional way – squeezing olive mash in a vertical tower press between fibre mats known as *scourtins*. The merits of each extraction system can be debated endlessly. What matters is that by both means, France produces some of the world's most enjoyable oils.

spain and portugal

*Some of the most enduring images of Spain and Portugal
are those of olive-dotted hillsides. Many massive,
venerable olive trees flourish alongside neat orchards
of well-pruned young trees, perfectly epitomizing both
tradition and progress.*

The relationship between human beings and the olive
is very ancient – there is a site in Spain where
archaeologists have found an olive stone carbon-dated
to 6000 BC. Since the fourth century BC, olives, olive
products and olive oil have all played a profound part in
Spain's history and development, her cultural stability
and European dominance.

By the first century BC, it was a major supplier of quality
olive oil for the entire Roman Empire. At that time it was
transported in large, elegant clay pots or amphorae,
each clearly marked with the grower's name, harvest
date, shipper's name and the olive type from which the
oil had been pressed.

Early records kept by the great estates sometimes
included the dates and planting history of each tree.
There are even records of trees that produced the oil
Christopher Columbus took on his first voyage to the
New World, and those trees are still bearing olives
today. By 1560, Spanish olive cuttings were taken to
Peru, and in the 1700s the Franciscans introduced the
olive into Mexico, then north into California.

Today, there are six designated denominations of origin
in Spain – Siurana and Les Garrigues, both in Catalonia,

and Sierra Mágina, Priego de Cordoba, Baena and Sierra de Segura in Andalucia. Each has its own unique characteristics, proudly defended and maintained, producing some of the most superb olive oils in the world.

Andalucia's oils are said to be strong in taste and intensity with a 'fruity shadow', an impressive power. Oils from northern Catalonia tend to be smoother, sweeter, but not spicy, with a scent of dried fruit and almonds in the afterglow. The almond scent may be the result of organic companion planting of olives and almond trees – a sound practice that is ancient but relevant still because it helps control fruit flies and other pests.

Today the gran *catadores*, Spain's master blenders, guarding their *trujales* (wells) of unfiltered oils, have a reputation second to none for their devotion to excellence. At the same time, Spain's olive oil industry seems to be developing at a steady rate.

The red soils, the rocks, the sloping undulations of olive-tree-dotted hills and valleys, the old dwellings inhabited for centuries – all seem to give a sense of unbroken continuity. Yet this is a country that has boldly embraced change – the new rationalized ways of production. As a result, Spain now produces some of the most magnificent oils in the world.

In Spain, meals traditionally end with olives. They form part of every tapas selection and the oil helps to begin each new day. A decade ago, when investigating olive oil, I found to my curiosity that many older Spaniards drink a spoonful of extra virgin olive oil each morning as a tonic, thought to be good for the digestion and for the heart (modern science has finally caught up with them there).

Portugal's olive oil is delicious and vigorously fruity, but for some people it can be an acquired taste, because the Portuguese usually prefer to keep their fruit for a week before it goes to the press. However, you can also find warmly fragrant, fruity, but not overly earthy oils, so perhaps this indicates a change in trend. Portugal is a prodigious consumer of the 'good oil' in its cuisine, and so imports olive oil from Spain in some considerable quantities.

greece: mainland and islands

Olive trees are virtually everywhere in Greece – in public squares, around monasteries, along city streets, in geometric grids over breathtakingly lovely valleys and hillsides. They are in the back gardens of nearly every house, often along with a fig tree, a grape vine and scented white jasmine.

From Aegina to Zakynthos, olive trees are deep-rooted in the Hellenic soil. The gift of the goddess Athena, olive oil is irrevocably intertwined with the culture and psyche of every Greek, from peasant to politician. Nowhere is the heritage of olive oil more linked with mythology and daily life than in Greece. The people consume, per capita, more olive oil than any other nation – more than the Spanish, more even than the Italians – and it is the world's third-largest producer.

It is 4,000 years since full-scale cultivation of the olive tree first began in Ancient Greece. There were laws to protect the trees: no olive wood could be traded and cutting down of trees was restricted. As Homer wrote, 'Olive oil is liquid gold' – particularly telling since this was written at a time when the rest of the Mediterranean was economically depressed.

Greece's 143 million olive trees are champion high-grade extra virgin producers – making 20 per cent of the total world production. In reality, much of Greece's wonderful oil is exported in bulk to other EU countries that cannot produce enough or have lots of refined olive oils in need of an upgrade provided by blending with Greece's good oil. So, because much Greek olive oil is marketed as 'Produce of Elsewhere', most of us have tasted it without knowing it. Labelling rules are being tightened, so it should now be indicated where the olives are grown, picked and pressed. Look out for Greek oil and help it enjoy the fame and popularity it richly deserves.

Generally, olives in Greece are picked by hand, stroked or beaten down with sticks, rakes and combs, often onto cloths spread under or hung below the trees. It is only the newer groves with level ground and accurately spaced trees that can support costly mechanization such as machine plucking.

In locations such as the southern Peloponnese, much production is carried out as it has been for centuries, with old stone presses still regularly in use. In some places, such as the Monastery of St Chrysopigi in Crete, olives are organically produced and the oil is soft and fruity with an elegant peppery 'bite'. In the Mani area, eco-tourism and agri-holidays are raising outsiders' awareness. Tourists have free lodging in return for picking the crop and sharing the conviviality of the harvest and its struggles.

Olive oil has always been the main fat source in Greece and, in ancient times, butter was thought fit only for barbarians. Even today, babies are baptized using olive oil. Many savoury dishes are dressed with olive oil and often just a squeeze of fresh lemon, a sprinkle of rigani (oregano), some salt and pepper – that's all. Salads, soups and even cakes and pastries are deliciously full of it. Greeks use it for deep-frying and that is the reason why even potato chips taste especially good in Greece.

north africa and the middle east

A Moroccan Berber tribesman may have been the first to coax the wild oleaster into an oil-bearing olive tree. Centuries before Christ, Ancient Greek colonists grew olives on the edge of the Sahara. Later, the Romans cultivated them along the North African coast, where they now form an integral part of the landscape.

Almost all the olive oil produced in North Africa is either consumed locally, or sold for blending on the international market. The Lebanon, Syria, Turkey and Israel are also significant producers, and all these countries have long historical links with olive cultivation.

Morocco is a huge exporter of olives, but less so of oil, while Tunisia is the largest producer of olive oil outside the EU. In reality, Tunisians and Moroccans tend to like their olive oil with up to 5 per cent acidity: this is strong and to many Western palates would be unacceptable.

Algeria and Libya consume a great part of what they produce and it is difficult to obtain any, even for a sample tasting, and it is rarely exported. Both countries import olive oil to satisfy home consumption.

Israel is a leader in the science and technology of cultivation but is not a big producer. Most production is needed for home use. Intensive modern techniques of organized planting, irrigation and harvesting, especially mechanized types, are constantly under review.

Syria and Turkey are the largest producers in the Middle East according to International Olive Oil Council figures. Many regions are covered with olive trees, often of advanced age and great beauty. They are an established element of the culture and families tend their olive trees lovingly. Many of the

pressing methods follow old rules: they are relaxed and fairly low-tech. New technology is on its way, but is not yet greatly advanced.

A small amount of excellent Palestinian olive oil is sold under the 'fair trade' and 'pesticide free' labels in the UK.

Similarly, a tiny volume of oil from the Lebanon is exported to Britain and the US, where there are Lebanese populations. War has not aided the expansion of the Lebanese industry but, since olives and good olive oil have always been valued by the people and played a major role in their superb cuisine, there can be some optimism for future development as the economy and trade recover.

california

Olive oil has been produced since the late eighteenth century at the missions in San Diego Alcalá set up by Spanish Franciscans. They used Mexican stock and these trees are still often used for grafting. The original trees probably arrived about 1785 and the first artisans in 1795. The padres used the oil for sacramental purposes, then for bartering.

In the US, olives have been grown for the table rather than for oil, but times are changing. California is the only state with a notable olive industry, especially in the Napa and Sonoma Valleys, although Arizona and Texas each produce a small amount.

After the missions were secularized (1834–36), farmers imported hundreds of olive varietals from Europe and planted them across the state. By 1880 there was a booming oil market. But about 1905, cheap vegetable oil began to flood the market and by the 1940s the heavy competition from cheaper imports of yet more oils caused a trade war and put most of the Californian producers out of business altogether.

Recently, partly initiated by olive oil's desirable, healthy image, there has been a new trend for quality oil production. Fifteen years ago there were about three fine olive oils – today there are over 50, pressed or extracted in more than 14 mills. Prices are naturally high for all these premium, cold-pressed, extra virgin olive oils.

At present, there is some variation in the styles of US olive oils, from buttery-mild, sweet and yellow types to spicier, even bitter, green fruity olive oils with a light peppery bite. This distinction may develop as palates grow more sophisticated and local producers in California try to emulate the best characteristics of highly desirable, estate-bottled extra virgins from Tuscany and Umbria – a passion for American gourmets over recent years.

US producers want a bigger share of the market for really classy, distinctive, extra virgin olive oils and they have the technology, expertise and the will to achieve that.

australia and
new zealand

These buoyant young countries, with wine industries that are the envy of the world, seem set for an exciting olive oil boom. Their oil producers, like their winemakers, label oils according to estate, region, variety, and year of pressing. The aim is to make premium quality oils to complement the vibrant local cuisines.

In Sydney or Auckland restaurants, as soon as you sit down, you're likely to be given a saucer of greeny-gold, locally produced olive oil rather than butter to taste with your fresh, warm, crusty bread.

Australia, with its sunny climate, massive spaces, horticultural infrastructure and innovative technology, has the will and the expertise to support a thoroughly enviable olive oil industry. It tests soils for nutrient status, plans olive groves for mechanical watering and harvesting efficiency and, nursing its 'clean green' image as New Zealand does, it hopes to be ecologically defensible too – an admirable stance.

Australia's first olive trees were brought in late December 1800 by George Suttor, a protégé of Sir Joseph Banks, the great botanist from Cook's expedition. But, in spite of the best efforts of visionaries, prison reformers, botanists, State governors and entrepreneurs, the olive oil industry never took off: it was an ongoing tale of boom, gloom and bust.

It was not until after World War II, with the influx of European immigrants from Italy, Greece, Turkey and the Lebanon, that the olive tree was properly treated and finally understood. It represented the best of 'home' to the new arrivals. Many were amazed to find a legacy of wild or feral olives, often along the roadsides, growing from bird-spread stones from colonial times. These were piquant and delicious. Now olive trees grow in a great southern band across the country, mostly in wine-growing areas, from the Margaret River in Western Australia to South Australia, Victoria, New South Wales and even South-east Queensland.

A properly cultivated, conventionally irrigated olive tree will produce, on average, a 50 kg yield. These figures were mind-boggling to people who came from the Mediterranean.

In New Zealand, the most prolific areas match the great wine areas. Olive groves stretch from northern North Island to Central Otago in the South Island. Many are boutique estates with their own pressing rooms, tasting facilities and shops selling olives, olive oil and associated products. High-tech facilities, often certified with the organic 'Bio-Gro' tag, produce small runs, often of special reserve quality.

Olive oil, no longer a curiosity sold in ethnic grocers, is now a condiment sold in every deli and supermarket, and found in most kitchen cupboards. We're going to hear more of Antipodean olive oil.

soups and salads

Soups and salads best display extra virgin's many charms. For soups, broths or chowders, sizzle a little garlic in olive oil at the start of cooking, or trickle extra virgin on top at serving time. A handful of lettuce is really only raw green leaves, but when you add a pool of extra virgin olive oil, it suddenly becomes a salad and takes on extra complexity to please the eye and the palate.

There are many versions of chowder; creamy New England style, tomato-based Manhattan style and dozens of variations around the world. But it is Boston clam chowder that I remember most fondly: spicy, hot and steaming with a pile of saltine crackers on the side. This version is easy to make and olive oil keeps it heart-healthy too: a bonus.

spicy clam chowder

4 tablespoons extra virgin olive oil

4 slices bacon, cut into strips or large cubes, about 75 g

1 kg live clams, well scrubbed

750 ml boiling fish or chicken stock

1 large onion, chopped

2–4 medium potatoes, cubed, about 400 g

3 celery stalks, sliced

2 teaspoons hot paprika

1 red chilli, deseeded and chopped

400 g canned chopped tomatoes

1 teaspoon sea salt flakes

leaves from 1 small bunch of flat leaf parsley, chopped

saltines, crackers, French bread or crusty rolls, to serve

Serves 6–8

Heat half the olive oil in a large frying pan, add the bacon and sauté until crisp. Remove with a slotted spoon. Add the clams and half the stock. Cover the pan and bring to the boil. Reduce the heat and simmer for 5 minutes or until the clams open.

Put wet muslin or wet kitchen paper in a sieve and pour the clams and their liquid through the sieve to strain out the sand. Reserve the cooking liquid and the clams.

Heat the remaining oil in the rinsed pan, add the onion, potatoes, celery, paprika and chilli and sauté for 5 minutes. Add the tomatoes, remaining stock and salt. Bring to the boil, reduce the heat and simmer for 10 minutes or until the vegetables are part-tender. Add the reserved cooking liquids, bacon and clams, stir gently, then simmer for 5–10 minutes until the flavours are well blended. Serve in deep, wide soup bowls, with parsley sprinkled on top.

Saltines (salted, crisp crackers) are the traditional accompaniment, but any salted crackers will do. French bread or crusty rolls are also suitable.

soupe au pistou

4 tablespoons extra virgin olive oil

350 g potatoes, cut into 1 cm cubes

1 leek, green and white parts cut into 1 cm rounds, about 200 g

2 carrots, cut into 1 cm slices

250 g pumpkin or butternut squash, cut into 1 cm cubes

2 courgettes, cut into 1 cm slices or cubes

100 g green beans, cut into 5 cm lengths

250 g tomatoes, skinned, deseeded and chopped

6 leaves spring cabbage, kale or cavolo nero cabbage (optional)

2 teaspoons salt, or to taste

250 g shelled fresh haricot beans, shelled broad beans or the canned equivalent, or 100 g dried beans, soaked then cooked

125 g dried pasta

Pistou paste

6 garlic cloves, chopped

1 teaspoon coarse sea salt

25 g fresh basil leaves

75 g freshly grated Parmesan cheese

125 ml extra virgin olive oil

Serves 4: makes 3 litres

Pistou – made with fresh basil and good olive oil, but without pine nuts – is the French equivalent of Italian pesto. In both countries, hearty vegetable soups or pasta are boosted by a dollop of this scented sauce. Served hot, they are cheering and sustaining. Cold, they are fresh and elegant.

Heat the oil in a large, heavy saucepan, add the potatoes, leek, carrots and pumpkin and sauté until part-tender and aromatic, about 10 minutes. Add 2 litres boiling water, then the courgettes, beans, tomatoes, cabbage, if using, fresh or canned haricot or broad beans, dry pasta and most of the salt. Bring to the boil, reduce the heat, part-cover with a lid and simmer for 20 minutes or until the vegetables are soft and the pasta cooked through. Taste, then add the remaining salt if needed.

Meanwhile to make the pistou, put the garlic, salt and basil in a blender or food processor and blend to a paste. With the motor running, add half the cheese and gradually pour in half the olive oil. Add the remaining cheese and oil all at once and blend one last time. It can also be made with a mortar and pestle. The paste should be a vivid green.

Serve hot or cool with a generous spoonful of the green paste on top. The pistou recipe makes 250 ml – use any leftovers for pasta, on char-grilled toast, with baked seafood or stirred into plain risotto.

In Greece and Italy, wonderful selections of baby green leaves and herbs are gathered from gardens and fields in spring and summer. All sorts of leaves are used – from wild samphire to dandelion greens, rocket, wild mustard, curly endive, purslane, radish and beetroot leaves. Many are also available here, so choose a mixture of leaves.

salad of wild greens

2 handfuls of peppery leaves, such as rocket or watercress

2 handfuls of bitter leaves, such as endive or frisée

2 handfuls of crisp lettuce, such as Little Gem, torn

1 small head of chicory, separated into leaves

1 small head of radicchio, separated into leaves

leaves from 1 small bunch of flat leaf parsley, dill or mint (optional)

1 small red onion, finely sliced into rings

Dressing

2 garlic cloves, crushed

½ teaspoon sea salt flakes

1–1½ tablespoons freshly squeezed lemon juice

4–6 tablespoons extra virgin olive oil, preferably Greek or Italian

Serves 4

To make the dressing, put the garlic, salt and half the lemon juice in a small bowl and mix with a hand-held stick blender. Trickle in the oil and blend until a rich emulsion forms. Taste, then add enough lemon juice to give bite.

Alternatively, use a mortar and pestle to pound the garlic and salt to a sticky paste. Trickle in the oil, continuing to pound and stir until a rich emulsion forms. Add lemon juice to taste.

Put the washed leaves, herbs, if using, and onion rings in a large bowl, cover with a plastic bag, seal and chill until ready to serve, so the leaves stay crisp and fresh.

Just before serving, trickle the dressing over the leaves and toss thoroughly with your hands or 2 wooden spoons.

Traditionally, North African couscous, a type of granulated semolina, is steamed over a tagine or stew. Today's 'instant' couscous is an easy substitute. Serve it hot or warm as an accompaniment for meat or poultry, or as a salad with cold, crisp greens such as chicory, watercress or rocket.

couscous with spicy fruits

Heat the oil in a saucepan, add the garlic and onion and sauté for 2 minutes. Crush the cumin and coriander seeds coarsely, then add to the pan. Add the paprika, stir and cook for about 1 minute more. Add the salt, stock, couscous, almonds and grapes. Stir again, return to the boil, reduce to low heat, add the figs, apricots or peaches, then cover with a lid.

Cook for 2 minutes then turn off the heat and leave the pan, covered, for 5 minutes, undisturbed. Uncover and fluff up the couscous with a fork – all the liquid should have been absorbed. Serve immediately.

Note Fresh apricots and some other stone fruits will brown and darken if left for any period after this type of cooking – the taste won't change, but the dish loses its glamour.

4 tablespoons extra virgin olive oil

2 garlic cloves, finely sliced

1 onion, sliced

½ teaspoon cumin seeds

½ teaspoon coriander seeds

½ teaspoon sweet paprika

½ teaspoon salt

500 ml boiling chicken stock

175 g 'instant' couscous

50 g flaked almonds, toasted in a dry frying pan

150 g grapes, halved

6 fresh figs or apricots or 2 peaches, cut in wedges and any stones removed

1 tablespoon harissa paste, to serve (optional)

Serves 4

A lovely exotic taste from Morocco – a salad with a flowery Moorish note in the dressing, made faintly hot and pink with spicy harissa paste. The softness of olive oil gives balance – an integral part of this colourful salad. Serve alone or as a side dish. Fez is one of the culinary capitals of Morocco, producing oil that is often spicy and fragrant, if somewhat strong.

fez orange salad
with olives and onions

4–6 large oranges, about 675 g

1 teaspoon orange flower water

1 teaspoon harissa paste

4 tablespoons extra virgin olive oil

2 red onions, finely sliced into rings

about 20 green olives stuffed with anchovies

about 20 dry-cured black olives

8 mint sprigs, to serve

Serves 4–6

Wash and dry the oranges and, using a zester or grater, remove about 1 tablespoon of zest shreds. Using a sharp knife, peel and discard the skin, pith and the outer membranes.

Slice the oranges crossways, reserving all the juices. Put the collected juices, orange flower water, harissa paste and olive oil in a bowl and whisk to form a pinky-red dressing. (If there doesn't seem to be enough juice, squeeze one of the orange slices and add its juices as well.) Put the sliced onions in a bowl, cover with boiling water, leave for 2 minutes, then drain. Refresh in a bowl of iced water, then drain again.

Arrange the sliced oranges in concentric circles on a flat platter. Add the onion rings and olives, trickle the dressing over the top, then add the orange zest and mint sprigs. Serve cool.

Italian *caprese* salad normally includes basil, but in this variation, rocket adds a curious, peppery bite. Do use superb, soft *mozzarella di bufala*, made from the rich, very white milk of water buffaloes. Add good tomatoes and an exceptional, unfiltered or estate-bottled, first-pressed extra virgin olive oil and this dish becomes sublime. Never refrigerate it: make just a few minutes before eating.

mozzarella, tomato and rocket salad

3 buffalo mozzarella cheeses, 150 g each

4 large tomatoes

4 handfuls of wild rocket

6–8 tablespoons unfiltered or estate-bottled, first-pressed extra virgin olive oil, preferably Italian

sea salt and freshly ground black pepper

crusty bread, to serve

Serves 4

Drain the mozzarellas. Slice thickly or pull them apart into big rough chunks, showing the grainy strands. Arrange down one side of a large serving platter.

Slice the tomatoes thickly and arrange them in a second line down the middle of the plate. If they are very large, cut them in half first, then into semi-circles. Add the rocket leaves down the other side of the platter.

Sprinkle with salt and pepper, then just before serving trickle the olive oil over the top. Make sure you have crusty bread (slightly char-grilled tastes good) to mop up the juices.

Variation Sharp, herby black olives may also be added.

antipasti and snacks

Delicious snacks and starters can only be improved when made with extra virgin olive oil. These taste treats are based on fresh, pickled, salted, dried or cured foods, or simple purées, dips and spreads. Extra virgin is every Mediterranean cook's favourite ingredient, and all these antipasti and informal snacks depend upon it for aroma, flavour and beauty.

This casual Australian dish originated in the Mediterranean. Good-quality local produce such as fish, prawns and other seafood have been given an elegant modern twist by the verve and talent of Aussie chefs. Sydney – where food and wine are almost a religion – must be one of the great culinary capitals of the world.

australian antipasto platter

Arrange small piles of cheese, caperberries, fennel and prawns on a large serving platter. Add a second row of nuts or olives, ham and figs.

Put the vine tomatoes on an oiled baking tray and roast in a preheated oven at 220°C (425°F) Gas 7 for 8–10 minutes or until blistered, soft, dark and aromatic. Add to the second row on the platter.

Put the soy sauce in a bowl, add half the oil and half the mint, then mash together. Trickle the mixture over the cheese, caperberries, fennel and prawns, then sprinkle with the remaining herbs and sesame seeds.

Use the remaining olive oil to sprinkle over the nuts or olives, ham, figs and roasted tomatoes. Serve cool within 30 minutes.

125 g mild goats' cheese or buffalo mozzarella, sliced or torn

4 tablespoons caperberries or capers, rinsed

1 fennel bulb, finely sliced lengthways

8 cooked king prawns or baby crayfish tails, in the shell, halved lengthways

4 tablespoons salted macadamia or pistachio nuts or black olives

4 slices Parma ham

4 fresh figs, halved lengthways

4 bunches of cherry tomatoes, on the vine

leaves from a small bunch of mint

2 teaspoons soy sauce or fish sauce

125 ml best-quality, estate-bottled, extra virgin olive oil

1 tablespoon toasted sesame seeds

an oiled baking tray

Serves 4

If your family or friends are lucky enough to own olive-producing trees, here is a small-scale home cure for spicy, fragrant green olives. Pick them midway through autumn when they are yellow-green but still hard. Some Italian and Greek greengrocers also sell them in season, and they may be found in Jewish delis.

syrian-style green olives

2 kg greenish-yellow, hand-picked olives, twigs and leaves removed

zest of 6 oranges, removed in long strips

500 g salt

4 tablespoons dried thyme, crumbled

4 tablespoons dried wild fennel, crumbled, or dill

1–2 tablespoons tiny dried hot red chillies

extra virgin olive oil, to cover

2 large preserving jars, sterilized

Makes 2 large jars

Put the cleaned olives in a large, non-metal container. Cover generously with cold water and leave for 4 days, changing the water every 24 hours.

Drain the olives, dry them with kitchen paper and spread out in a single layer on a sheet of thick plastic. Let dry naturally for several hours longer.

Arrange the long strips of orange zest on wire racks and bake in a preheated oven at 180°C (350°F) Gas 4 for about 12–18 minutes or until brittle. Put two-thirds in a food processor and grind to a coarse powder. Mix with the salt, thyme and fennel, then sprinkle over the olives. Set aside for 24 hours.

Next day, pack the olives into 2 large sterilized jars, tucking in the remaining bits of zest and the chillies. Cover with extra virgin olive oil. Seal, label and store in a cool, dark, dry place. They will be ready to use after 1 week.

A simple, delicious snack, with mellow olive oil accentuating the flavours. Some frugal cooks score and salt aubergines in the hope that less oil will be required. A curious debate, centuries old.

aubergine antipasto
with pine nuts and herbs

2–3 medium aubergines, about 750 g

2 tablespoons sea salt

125 ml extra virgin olive oil

1 small bunch of mint, half chopped, half in sprigs

1 small bunch of flat leaf parsley, half chopped, half in sprigs

2 tablespoons aged balsamic vinegar

50 g pine nuts

sea salt and freshly ground black pepper

a stove-top grill pan

Serves 4–6

Slice the aubergines lengthways into 1 cm slices. Score both sides of each slice with a fork. Sprinkle with salt. Let drain on a rack for 20 minutes, then pat dry with kitchen paper.

Meanwhile heat a stove-top grill pan until very hot. Wipe with olive oil using a wad of crumpled kitchen paper or a heatproof brush. Paint each slice of aubergine with olive oil. Arrange on the hot pan, pressing down firmly. Cook for 3–5 minutes each side until grill-marked, tender and aromatic. Heat 1 tablespoon olive oil in a frying pan, add the pine nuts and toast gently until golden. Remove from the pan and set aside.

Scatter the cooked aubergine with chopped mint, chopped parsley, pepper and a few drops of balsamic vinegar. Loop the slices on serving plates, add the pine nuts and sprigs of mint and parsley and serve as an antipasto.

Note If you grow your own aubergines and/or know they are the modern, hot-house-raised non-bitter type, omit the salting process and continue with the recipe.

Versions of this handsome, delicious dish are found all over Spain, the Basque country and the South of France. Geographical origins dictate the exact ingredients – but peppers, garlic, tomatoes, ham and often eggs are essentials, as is fruity, robust olive oil. A good earthy Spanish oil would suit it well.

piperrada

4 tablespoons extra virgin olive oil

1 Spanish onion, sliced into rings

3 garlic cloves, sliced

2 red peppers, halved, deseeded and sliced

2 yellow peppers, halved, deseeded and sliced

2 ripe red tomatoes, skinned and sliced

6 eggs

4 slices jamon serrano or Parma ham

1 dried red chilli, crumbled (optional)

sea salt and freshly ground black pepper

Serves 6–8

Heat 3 tablespoons of the oil in a heavy frying pan over medium heat. Add the onions and garlic and sauté until soft and fragrant but not browned. Add the peppers and tomatoes. Cover the pan, reduce the heat and cook to form a soft, thick purée, 8–12 minutes. Add salt and pepper to taste.

Break the eggs into a bowl, add salt and pepper and stir with a fork. Using a spatula, push a space clear near the centre of the pan. Add the remaining oil to the space, then pour in the eggs. Stir gently over medium heat until semi-set. Turn off the heat.

Fold the slices of ham into rosettes or pleats, then add to the pan. Crumble over some dried chilli, if using, and serve straight from the pan.

Note Rounds or triangles of bread fried in olive oil are often served with piperrada.

sweet potato frittata

This Antipodean frittata, a sort of free-form omelette,
is made special by the golden sweetness of kumara
(a New Zealand variety of orange sweet potato), plus a
boost of garlic and parsley and the fruity ripeness of
good olive oil. It can be served alone, piled onto crusty
bread, toasted baguette, char-grilled ciabatta, or rolled
up inside a soft flatbread such as lavash.

1–2 orange sweet potatoes
(kumara)

1 small bunch of flat leaf
parsley, coarsely chopped

2–3 garlic cloves, chopped

6 free-range eggs

4 tablespoons virgin or extra
virgin olive oil, Antipodean
if possible

sea salt and freshly ground
black pepper

bread, toast or flatbread,
to serve

Serves 4–6

Bake the sweet potatoes in a preheated oven at 180°C
(350°F) Gas 4 for 30 minutes. Alternatively steam them or
cook in a microwave – prick with a fork and cook on HIGH
for 8–10 minutes, turning them over once.

Put the parsley, garlic, eggs, salt and pepper in a bowl and
stir briefly with a fork, barely mixing the yolks and whites.
Heat half the oil in a large, non-stick frying pan or 4 small
blini pans. Slice the sweet potato and add to the pan. Fry
at high heat, without stirring, for about 2 minutes, then turn
the slices over. Keeping the heat high, pour in the egg
mixture. Let cook undisturbed, until the edges bubble and
cling, then push the mixture around in the pan like
scrambled eggs, until almost completely set but still soft.
Serve hot with bread, toast or flatbread.

pan amb tomaquet

4 large, thick slices
country-style bread

1 large, very ripe
tomato

2 garlic cloves,
halved

6–8 thin slices
jamon serrano or
Parma ham

3–4 tablespoons
extra virgin olive oil

sea salt

Serves 4–6

Catalonia's favourite snack is bread – toasted or not – rubbed with garlic and roughly crushed tomato, then trickled with local olive oil and sprinkled with salt.

Toast, grill, char-grill or barbecue the bread briefly on both sides, so that it is crusty outside, soft inside. Rub one side of each slice with garlic. Pull or cut the tomato in half and rub the cut sides over the garlic side of each toast. Cube the tomato.

Top the toasts with loosely gathered folds of jamon serrano or Parma ham. Trickle oil generously all over each one and serve immediately. Serve plain or with tomato cubes on top.

bruschetta con funghi e formaggio

Superb, dense, green-gold olive oil is crucial for this dish. The first taste of freshly pressed local oil on bread is still a pleasure, but was once a staple.

Grill, toast or barbecue the bread on both sides. While still hot, quickly rub the garlic directly over one surface, discarding the skin as the flesh wears down. Trickle over enough olive oil to soak into the hot, garlicky toasts. Arrange the mushroom slices over one half of each piece and add a smear of cheese over the other. Add salt and pepper and serve immediately.

8 slices Italian country-style
bread, cut 2.5 cm thick

4–6 garlic cloves, crushed but
not peeled

6–8 tablespoons Italian extra
virgin olive oil

250 g mushrooms preserved
in oil, such as porcini,
drained and sliced

250 g Gorgonzola or dolcelatte
cheese

sea salt and freshly ground
black pepper

Serves 4 or 8

sauces, dips and dressings

Vinaigrette and mayonnaise, pesto and taramasalata – where would we be without these classic sauces, dips and dressings? Don't forget: olive oil, served quite alone, is the dressing *par excellence*. Keep a lively range of olive oil on your shelves – blends and varietals, peppery or sweetly mellow – and use them generously.

The simplest dressing can be just best-quality extra virgin poured over beautiful salad leaves, then a few drops of balsamic vinegar. At the other end of the spectrum can be an emulsion of oil, vinegar and seasonings mixed with additions such as mustard, cream or garlic. Instead of vinegar, you can use other acidic ingredients such as citrus juices. A vinaigrette can be almost anything you want it to be – even warmed – but even so, classic is often best.

classic vinaigrette

75 ml white or red wine vinegar (1 part)

375 ml extra virgin olive oil (5 parts)

sea salt and freshly ground white pepper

Makes 450 ml

Put all the ingredients in a bowl, vinaigrette flask or screw-top jar. Whisk, beat or shake to form a temporary emulsion. Store in a cool, dark place – bright sunlight and heat can turn it rancid. Use immediately or within a week – and shake again to mix.

To make a smaller amount – enough for one salad – use 1 part vinegar to 5 parts oil, plus salt and pepper to taste. You can also pour the ingredients into the salad bowl and beat them with a fork. Put the salad on top and leave undisturbed (no longer than 30 minutes), then toss just before serving.

Italy calls it *pesto*, France calls it *pistou* – wherever they come from, this family of sauces is a basic mixture of fresh herbs mixed to a paste with garlic, salt and good olive oil.

classic pesto

100 g pine nuts

125 ml extra virgin olive oil

6 garlic cloves, chopped

1 teaspoon coarse sea salt

25 g fresh basil leaves, torn

50 g freshly grated Parmesan cheese

50 g freshly grated pecorino cheese

Makes about 375 g

Put the pine nuts in a small frying pan, add 1 teaspoon of the olive oil and stir-fry quickly until golden. Remove and let cool.

Put the pine nuts, garlic, salt and basil in a food processor and work to a paste. Alternatively, use a mortar and pestle.

Still working, add half the cheese, then gradually pour in half the olive oil. Add the remaining cheese and oil all at once and work or blend one last time. The paste should be a vivid green.

simple mayonnaise

2 egg yolks, at room temperature

2 teaspoons Dijon mustard

¼ teaspoon salt

2 teaspoons fresh lemon juice or white wine vinegar

200 ml extra virgin olive oil

175 ml light oil, such as grapeseed, safflower or sunflower oil

Makes 400 ml

Homemade mayonnaise is so much better than any store-bought. It is one of the serendipities of the kitchen. You can vary it at will.

Put the yolks in a bowl with high, straight sides and curved base. Stir in the mustard, salt and half the lemon juice or vinegar and beat until smooth. Mix the oils in a small jug, then, with the oil jug in one hand and a hand-held electric whisk in the other, gradually trickle in the oil, whisking continuously to form a stiff, glossy emulsion. When all the oil has been added, taste, then whisk in the remaining juice or vinegar. Add salt to taste. Cover the surface with clingfilm until ready to use. It is best used immediately, it may also be refrigerated for up to 3 days.

This exciting, incendiary condiment is available in cans or jars in delicatessens and at good grocers, but homemade is also wonderful.

harissa paste

30 g large dried chillies, deseeded

2 large red peppers, char-grilled, skinned, deseeded and chopped

4 garlic cloves, crushed

½–1 teaspoon salt

2 tablespoons cumin seeds, coarsely crushed

2 tablespoons coriander seeds, coarsely crushed

2 tablespoons mild paprika

125 ml extra virgin olive oil

Makes 300 ml

Put the chillies in a bowl and cover with about 500 ml boiling water. Set aside to rehydrate, about 30 minutes.

Drain the chillies (reserving 2 tablespoons of soaking liquid) and scissor-snip them directly into a blender. Add the peppers, garlic, salt, cumin, coriander and paprika. Add the reserved soaking liquid and 5–6 tablespoons olive oil. Blend until smooth and creamy. Pour into small, sterilized jars with non-metal lids – they can be sterilized in the oven or a microwave. When cool, pour over a thin layer of olive oil. Seal with plastic or rubber lids or seals. Refrigerate for up to 2 weeks or freeze for up to 1 month.

Greek yoghurt is so rich, sharp and solid that it's almost like cheese. If you can't find the real thing, strain plain yoghurt through a muslin-lined sieve.

tzatziki

Grate the cucumber coarsely, put in a non-metal bowl, sprinkle with the salt, stir and let stand for 10 minutes. Put in a non-metal sieve and press hard to squeeze out the salt and liquid. Do not rinse. Return to a clean bowl and stir in the garlic and yoghurt. Spoon into small serving dishes and trickle a little olive oil on top. Serve with chopped herbs, black olives, bread, cucumber and carrot.

250 g cucumber, unpeeled

2 teaspoons salt

3 garlic cloves, crushed

375 ml strained plain Greek yoghurt

4 tablespoons extra virgin olive oil

To serve (optional)

fresh mint or parsley, chopped

black olives

bread

cucumber, cut in strips

carrots, cut in strips

Serves 4–6, makes about 700 ml

200 g dried chickpeas or 400 g cooked or canned

freshly squeezed juice of 1 lemon

2 garlic cloves, crushed

¼ teaspoon salt and freshly ground black pepper, plus extra to taste

2 tablespoons tahini paste (optional)

125 ml first-pressing extra virgin olive oil

To serve (optional)

paprika

olive oil

Serves 6–8: makes 400 ml

hoummus

Lemony, fresh hoummus and *hoummus bi tahini* (containing toasted sesame seed paste) are delicious Middle Eastern snack foods.

If using dried chickpeas, put in a bowl and cover with boiling water for 3 hours (or in cold water for 8 hours). Drain. Put in a large saucepan, cover with boiling water, bring to the boil, part-cover with a lid and simmer for 1½–2½ hours or until the chickpeas are easily crushable and tender. Drain.

Put the chickpeas in a food processor with the lemon juice, garlic, salt, pepper and tahini paste, if using. Blend briefly to a mousse. With the machine running, pour the oil through the feed tube to form a creamy purée. Add salt and pepper to taste. Serve cool or chilled, sprinkled with paprika or olive oil, if using.

Although this delicious, intense black paste began life in the South of France as a dip or spread for bread, today it is often used as a sauce for fish or folded through other emulsion sauces, purées or pasta to give a Mediterranean flavour. Capers, anchovies and tuna are essentials and Cognac adds particular pungency. Do not modify this recipe: it is meant to be powerfully strong and piquant.

tapenade

350 g salt-cured black olives, pitted (250 g after pitting)

50 g canned anchovies

100 g canned tuna in olive oil, drained

3 garlic cloves, crushed

½ teaspoon dried oregano or marjoram

50 g pickled or salted capers, drained

60 ml extra virgin olive oil, preferably Provençal

2 tablespoons Cognac

sea salt and freshly ground black pepper

bread, vegetable crudités or baked seafood, to serve

Serves 4–6: makes 500 ml

Put the pitted olives, anchovies, tuna, garlic, oregano, capers, salt and pepper in a food processor or mortar and pestle. Work to a messy paste, then trickle the oil through the feed tube, in pulsing bursts. Add salt and pepper to taste. Add half of the Cognac and purée again.

Spoon into a bowl and spoon the remaining Cognac over the top. Serve with crusty bread, garlicky bread, crostini, breadsticks, crisp vegetable crudités or baked seafood.

Note Do not even consider using the pre-pitted, unripe, dyed black olives sometimes available from the USA. Proper tree-ripened black olives, pitted at home, are essential.

2 tablespoons pressed salted cod's roe, uncoloured, or 110 g smoked cod's roe

50 g stale bread, wetted, squeezed dry, then crumbled

freshly squeezed juice of ½ lemon

1 large garlic clove, crushed (optional)

250 ml extra virgin olive oil, preferably Greek

4 tablespoons chopped red onion, blanched

To serve (optional)

black olives

fennel or celery, radishes or lettuce

warmed pita breads

Serves 6–8: makes 400 ml

Real, homemade taramasalata is a revelation. It is eons away from the lurid, tasteless, manufactured variety. Salted cod's roe is sold in Greek delis.

taramasalata

Put the cod's roe, bread, lemon juice and garlic, if using, in a food processor. Purée in brief bursts. With the machine running, pour in the oil, very slowly, through the feed tube, to form a pale, dense emulsion. With the machine still running, very gradually trickle in 3–4 tablespoons boiling water to lighten the mixture. Stir in the onions. Serve with black olives, raw fennel or crisp celery pieces, radishes or lettuce hearts and some warmed pita breads, torn.

Note If making with a mortar and pestle, omit the bread.

vegetables

The vegetables of the Mediterranean might have been specially designed to be teamed with olive oil. Aubergines and peppers, tomatoes and a whole raft of other vegetables – every one of them benefits from a libation of the holy oil. To roast red onions, to deep-fry potatoes or fritto misto, or simply to trickle over the finished product, vegetables and olive oil are health personified.

Deep-frying in batter is almost an endangered species of home cooking: health zealots urge caution or forbid it completely. However, minimal oil is absorbed if the temperatures are right and, in any case, olive oil does not degrade at high frying temperatures: a bonus since most other oils are damaged by this treatment.

vegetable fritto misto

4 courgettes, sliced into thin ribbons with a vegetable peeler

8 baby spinach leaves

8 sprigs of flat leaf parsley

8 spring onions, halved crossways

8 baby asparagus spears

8 okra (ladies' fingers), stalk ends trimmed slightly

2 lemons, halved

olive oil, for deep-frying

lemon chunks, to serve (optional)

Batter

250 g plain flour

3 tablespoons olive oil

3 egg whites

¼ teaspoon salt

an electric deep-fryer (optional)

Serves 4–6

Wash and dry all the vegetables with kitchen paper. If using okra, trim off the brown stalk ends only, so that none of the interior is exposed. Heat a deep-fryer or heavy saucepan with a frying basket and add 10 cm of olive oil ready for heating.

To make the batter, sift the flour into a large bowl. Beat 350 ml warm water with the olive oil in a second bowl, then whisk the mixture into the flour to give a creamy batter. Set aside for about 20 minutes.

Meanwhile pour the olive oil into a deep-fryer or a saucepan fitted with a chip basket. Heat the oil to 200°C (395°F) or until a 1 cm cube of bread browns in about 30 seconds.

Whisk the egg whites and salt together in a separate straight-sided bowl, then fold the mixture gently through the batter.

Using tongs or a skewer, dip each piece of vegetable into the batter, then fry in batches until crisp, golden and vividly green. Remove and drain on crumpled kitchen paper and keep hot while you fry the remaining vegetables. Serve hot with chunks of lemon.

This is not a recipe in which you would squander a fine, estate-bottled oil. But I – and many chefs – swear by commercial grades of extra virgin olive oil for deep-frying – these include some supermarket types. They are made by blending several grades of virgin and extra virgin oils from different sources to give a uniform but good taste, standard and price.

potato chips
pommes frites

1 kg floury potatoes, washed, peeled and dried

1.25 litres virgin olive oil, for frying

sea salt flakes

an electric deep-fryer (optional)

Serves 4

Cut the potatoes lengthways into 1.5 cm slabs, then slice the slabs lengthways to make even chips, 1.5 cm thick. Keep them in a large bowl of iced water until ready for cooking.

Meanwhile, pour the olive oil into a deep-fryer or heavy saucepan fitted with a frying basket. Heat to 160°C (312°F). Drain the chips and pat them dry.

Fry in batches until pale blond in colour, about 5 minutes. Drain each batch and set aside on kitchen paper while you cook the next one.

When all the chips are part-cooked to the pale blond stage, raise the heat to 190°C (375°F). Fry the chips for a second time, in batches, for 2 minutes, shaking the basket now and then, until they are deep gold, crisp and aromatic.

As each batch is cooked, drain them and shake out onto a plate lined with crumpled kitchen paper. (They should rustle when you tip them out.) Sprinkle with salt and eat without delay.

Note Never leave a pan of hot oil unattended, or within the reach of children.

This delicious dish, in one form or another, crops up all around the Mediterranean. In Italy, it may be piled on top of pizza; in Spain, especially Catalonia, it is served as a dish in its own right.

catalan spinach
with garlic, pine nuts and raisins

2 tablespoons extra virgin olive oil, preferably Spanish

3 tablespoons pine nuts

2 garlic cloves, crushed

6 canned anchovy fillets, chopped

500 g well-washed spinach, water still clinging

3 tablespoons seedless raisins

sea salt and freshly ground black pepper

Serves 3–4

Heat the oil in a non-stick frying pan. Carefully add the pine nuts, stir-fry for about 1 minute until golden, then remove quickly with a slotted spoon or drain through a sieve, reserving the oil and returning it to the pan.

Add the garlic and anchovies to the pan and mash them together over medium heat until aromatic, then add the wet spinach and raisins. Toss carefully with non-stick tongs or wooden spoons until evenly distributed. Cover the pan and cook over medium heat for 2–3 minutes, stirring halfway through. Uncover the pan, sprinkle with the pine nuts and toss well. Add salt and pepper to taste and serve hot or warm.

It can be served with garlicky toasts, sprinkled with olive oil or in warmed crusty rolls with slivers of cheese.

I was taught this elegant, curious dish by a dear friend in Paris two decades ago. The confit is excellent used as a short-term preserve and salad to accompany pickled herring, smoked salmon, and rich meats such as cold pork, ham, duck or goose, or indeed any charcuterie. Sealed, it will keep well for several days in the refrigerator.

500 g carrots, peeled

4 tablespoons caster sugar

2 teaspoons coriander seeds, crushed

½ teaspoon salt

1 small onion, finely sliced into rings

4 tablespoons fresh lemon, orange or lime juice

4 tablespoons extra virgin olive oil

flat leaf parsley, chervil or chives, to serve (optional)

Serves 4–8: makes 750 ml

carrot confit

Cut the carrots into thin rounds. Put them in a medium saucepan, add boiling water until just covered, then add the sugar, coriander seeds, salt and onion. Bring to the boil, stir gently, reduce the heat, part-cover and simmer for 6–8 minutes, stirring now and then until the carrots are vividly orange and tender and the liquid reduced slightly.

Stir in the citrus juice and olive oil. Add salt to taste. Turn off the heat. Turn the carrots gently in the liquid but do not break them: their prettiness is part of the charm.

Serve hot, warm or cool, sprinkled with herbs if you prefer. Alternatively, cool completely, transfer to sterilized glass jars or other covered containers, chill and use within 3 days.

A classic Spanish dish full of country richness and sweet summer bounty, although it is still possible to make it well into late autumn. It can be served as a hot, warm or cool salad, depending on your preference, and is grand and handsome, especially if accompanied by some country bread and a lively Spanish wine such as Rioja or rosado.

spanish roasted vegetable salad

2 red peppers

2 yellow peppers

½ butternut squash or 500 g pumpkin, unpeeled

2 red onions, unpeeled

2 Spanish onions, unpeeled

4 medium vine-ripened tomatoes

125 ml extra virgin olive oil, preferably Spanish

sea salt and freshly ground black pepper

Serves 4–6

Cut the peppers in half lengthways, slicing through the stems. Leave these intact but discard the pith and seeds.

Slice the butternut or pumpkin into 2.5 cm discs or chunks.

Cut the onions crossways into halves, leaving the roots and tops intact. Leave the skins on too – they give extra colour and flavour and protect the shape, though they are not eaten.

Put all the vegetables, cut sides up, in a large, lightly oiled roasting tin. Pour half the oil over the vegetables and sprinkle with salt and pepper.

Roast towards the top of a preheated oven at 240°C (475°F) Gas 9 for 30 minutes, until the vegetables are frizzled, fragrant, wrinkled and soft.

Pour the remaining oil over the top and serve hot, warm or cool. Eat the salad with your fingers, discarding the skins, roots and stems along the way.

Note Use bread to scoop up the sweet, oily, sticky juices from the hot tin – superb.

pasta, pizza, grains and beans

From time immemorial, the staple foods of the Mediterranean have been embellished with olive oil. The result is a plethora of lusty pasta dishes, risotto and crusty baked gnocchi, pizza and breads, and inspired uses for peas, beans and lentils – fresh and dried – all seasoned with aromatics, herbs and green-gold oil.

pappardelle with seafood sauce

500 g *tipo 00* flour (from Italian delicatessens)*

5 free-range medium eggs

2 teaspoons sea salt flakes, crushed

extra flour or semolina flour, for shaping

180 ml extra virgin olive oil, warmed

450 g lobster meat, from 1 kg whole lobster, or prawn or crab meat

1 bunch of fresh dill, chopped, about 40 g

1 bunch of fresh chives, chopped, about 40 g

shredded zest and juice of 1 lemon

sea salt and freshly crushed black pepper

Serves 4

* *If you make your own pasta, use this special Italian fine-grade flour. If utterly unobtainable, use plain flour instead.*

Put the flour, eggs and the 2 teaspoons sea salt in a food processor. Pulse for about 1 minute until the mixture comes together in a crumbly mass, then into a rough ball. Knead it firmly together and remove to a floured work surface.

Knead by hand for 2 minutes, then wrap in clingfilm and chill for 1 hour. Divide the dough into 4 parts, keeping 3 still wrapped. Starting on the thickest setting of the pasta machine, roll 1 piece of dough through, 3–4 times, folding the 2 ends into the middle each time to get a plump envelope of dough and giving it a half turn each time. Lightly flour the dough on both sides.

Roll it through all the settings on the pasta machine, starting at the thickest, about 6 times in all, until you get a 1 metre length of pasta (cut in half if it's easier). Hang over a chair or pole to air-dry. Continue until all the pasta sheets are lined up. Roll up each length, then slice into 2.5 cm wide ribbons (pappardelle). Unroll, dust in semolina flour, then cut each in half, to make strips about 50 cm long. Fill a large saucepan with hot water, add a pinch of salt and bring to the boil.

Meanwhile, to make the sauce, warm the oil in a heavy frying pan. Add the lobster meat, dill, chives, 1 tablespoon of the lemon juice, salt and pepper. Heat briefly until the flavours blend well. Leave on a very low heat to keep warm.

Add the pasta to the boiling salted water, cook for 1½ minutes, then drain in a colander. Tip the pasta into the sauce, toss gently with 2 wooden spoons, add the lemon zest and serve in pasta bowls.

Virtuoso Sicilian olive oil, plus assertive Mediterranean vegetables, produce a substantial pasta dish. No long simmering here: the tiny tomato halves are oven-roasted and the cubes of aubergine salted, then sautéed, to intensify the tastes. Handfuls of basil are the final flourish.

sicilian spaghetti

400 g dried pasta, such as spaghettini

1 aubergine, about 350 g, cut into 1 cm cubes

500 g mini plum tomatoes, halved and deseeded

125 ml extra virgin olive oil

125 ml tomato passata or tomato juice

2 garlic cloves, chopped

sea salt and freshly ground black pepper

leaves from 1 large bunch of fresh basil, to serve

Serves 4

Bring a large saucepan of salted water to the boil, ready to add the pasta when the vegetables are half cooked.

Put the aubergine cubes in a non-metal bowl, then add 1 teaspoon salt and set aside while you cook the tomatoes.

Pack the tomatoes, cut sides up, on an oven tray, sprinkle with the remaining salt and pour over 2 tablespoons of the oil. Roast in a preheated oven at 230°C (450°F) Gas 8 for 10 minutes or until wilted and aromatic.

Cook the pasta according to the packet instructions (about 8–12 minutes, depending on type).

Drain the aubergine and pat dry with kitchen paper. Heat 4 tablespoons of the olive oil in a non-stick frying pan. Add the aubergine and cook, stirring, over high heat until frizzled and soft, about 8 minutes. Add the roasted tomato halves, passata or juice, garlic and black pepper. Cook, stirring, for 2–3 minutes, then tear up most of the basil leaves and stir them through. Test the pasta for doneness and drain in a colander.

Return to the saucepan and toss in the remaining olive oil. Divide between heated bowls, spoon over the sauce, add a few fresh basil leaves and serve.

Penne rigate is one of the most useful dried pastas. Its ridged (*rigate*) surface and short, sharp shape is strong enough to hold large quantities of sauce. The oils of Tuscany, with their frequently assertive, peppery flavours, are well-suited for use with pasta, and sometimes you need nothing more in the way of a dressing.

penne rigate
with saffron and cracked pepper

Bring a large saucepan of salted water to the boil, then add the pasta in a steady stream. Stir, then cook, uncovered, at a gentle boil for 9 minutes or until *al dente*.

Meanwhile, using a mortar and pestle, grind the saffron and 1 teaspoon sea salt to a powder. Add the eau de vie or hot water and stir to dissolve.

Heat 3 tablespoons of the oil in a heavy frying pan. Add the garlic and leek and sauté for 2–3 minutes. Add the saffron liquid, cheese and wine. Mash and stir to form a creamy sauce. Simmer, stirring, until the wine loses its raw taste and the flavours have mellowed, about 3 minutes.

Drain the pasta, toss into the sauce and stir until coated. Serve topped with the Parmesan curls, cracked pepper, salad leaves and sprinkled with the remaining oil.

500 g dried penne rigate

a large pinch of saffron threads or ¼ teaspoon powdered saffron

2 tablespoons grappa or other eau de vie

125 ml extra virgin olive oil, preferably Tuscan

2 garlic cloves, finely sliced

1 leek, white only, finely sliced

250 g low-fat soft cheese, cream cheese or a mixture

125 ml white wine

50 g Parmesan cheese, freshly shaved into curls

sea salt and cracked black pepper

4–6 baby radicchio or trevise leaves, to serve

Serves 4

french ravioles with herb and cheese filling

250 g plain flour

2 eggs, 1 separated

4 tablespoons extra virgin olive oil

½ teaspoon salt

1.25 litres boiling chicken stock, for poaching

Filling

2 tablespoons extra virgin olive oil

8 tablespoons chopped fresh parsley, about 25 g

4 tablespoons chopped fresh chives, about 10 g

4 spring onions, finely chopped

100 g soft goats' cheese

8 tablespoons freshly grated Gruyère cheese

To serve

extra virgin olive oil, warmed

freshly grated Gruyère cheese (optional)

a plain biscuit cutter, 7.5 cm in diameter

Serves 4 as a main course or 8 as a starter

These are not Italian but French – old-fashioned and curiously appetizing. They originate in the Dauphiné region, famous for its dairy products, so serve the ravioles sprinkled with extra cheese.

Put the flour, 1 egg, 1 egg white and the oil in a food processor. Blend for 1 minute. Add 1½ tablespoons water and process to a stiff ball of dough. Wrap in clingfilm and chill.

To make the filling, heat the oil in a frying pan, add the parsley, chives and spring onions and sauté for 2 minutes. Stir in the egg yolk and cook until set. Stir in the goats' cheese and Gruyère, then let cool or chill.

Using a rolling pin on a floured work surface, roll out the dough thinly to about 3 mm thickness. Using the biscuit cutter, cut out 48 circles, covering them as you cut.

Put 1 teaspoon of filling in the middle of one circle and brush the edges of the dough with water. Top with a second circle of dough and crimp with a fork to seal. Repeat until all the dough circles and all the filling have been used: you should have 24.

Put the stock in a large saucepan and bring to the boil. Add 8 of the ravioles at a time and poach for 4–5 minutes until tender, translucent and floating. Remove with a slotted spoon, put in a bowl and keep hot until all the ravioles have been cooked. Serve with a little warmed olive oil trickled over the top and sprinkled with extra Gruyère, if using.

I prefer these semolina-based gnocchi to the potato version. The dough is stiffer and can be cut out with a biscuit cutter. They can be baked or microwaved until crusty with two kinds of cheese. Olive oil is used to make the dough and also poured over at serving time.

oven-baked semolina gnocchi

2 tablespoons extra virgin olive oil

8 level tablespoons coarse semolina, about 90 g, plus extra for shaping

100 g Parmesan cheese, freshly grated

100 g Gruyère cheese, freshly grated or finely cubed

1 handful of flat leaf parsley, coarsely chopped

¼ teaspoon grated nutmeg

¼ – ½ teaspoon crumbled dried red chilli (optional)

sea salt

4 tablespoons first-pressed extra virgin olive oil, to serve

a plain biscuit cutter, 5 cm in diameter

a small baking dish, lightly oiled

Serves 2–3

Put 250 ml warm water in a large heatproof bowl or jug. Add the oil, ½ teaspoon salt and semolina in that order and whisk until well mixed. The oil helps avoid lumps, but work quickly.

Microwave on HIGH, uncovered, for 3 minutes, stirring once. Alternatively, pour into a non-stick frying pan and cook, stirring constantly with a wooden spoon over moderate heat until the mixture thickens and forms a panade or paste, about 3 minutes. It will come away from the sides.

Stir in half the Parmesan, half the Gruyère, and all the parsley, nutmeg and chilli, if using. Tip out the dough onto a work surface dusted with semolina. Pat and smooth out the paste to a square about 20 x 20 cm. Using the biscuit cutter, cut out 16 rounds. Lift them out carefully with a spatula.

Arrange in a small, lightly oiled baking dish in overlapping concentric circles or rows. Sprinkle with the remaining Parmesan and Gruyère and half the olive oil. Microwave again on HIGH, uncovered, for 2 minutes or bake in a preheated oven at 200°C (400°F) Gas 6 for 30–35 minutes or until hot, crusty and aromatic. Serve immediately, sprinkled with the remaining olive oil.

baby pizzas
with assorted toppings

500 g unbleached plain flour

2 sachets easy-blend dried yeast, 7 g each

1 teaspoon salt

4 tablespoons extra virgin olive oil

Toppings

250 ml fresh tomato sauce, passata, tapenade or sun-dried tomato pesto

250 ml wilted fresh spinach, rocket or roasted peppers

100 g black olives and/or capers

50 g anchovies, halved lengthways and/ or toasted pine nuts

250 g fresh mozzarella cheese, drained and cubed

8 garlic cloves, chopped

1–2 tablespoons chopped fresh rosemary, sage or thyme

250 ml extra virgin olive oil

sea salt flakes and freshly ground black pepper

2 baking sheets, lightly oiled

a round biscuit cutter, 5–7.5 cm in diameter

Serves 8: makes 32–40

Everyone seems to enjoy pizza and these tiny ones, made with whatever topping selection you choose, are also good to serve at a party.

To make the dough, put the flour, yeast and salt in a food processor. Pulse briefly to sift the dry ingredients. Add the olive oil and 360 ml lukewarm water. Process in short bursts for 15 seconds to form a soft mass, not a ball.

Transfer to a floured work surface, then knead by hand for 2 minutes, slamming down the dough 2–3 times. Put the dough in a clean, oiled bowl. Turn it over once to coat with oil. Put the bowl of dough in a large plastic bag, seal and let rise until doubled in size, about 1½ hours in a warm place.

Put the dough on the work surface and punch it down with oiled hands. Divide into 2. Pat and roll out each piece to a circle about 5 mm thick. Push dimples all over it with your fingers.

Using the biscuit cutter, cut out about 16 pizzetta shapes. Set them on a baking sheet. Top each one with ½–1 teaspoon of sauce, paste or pureé. Add spinach, rocket or roasted peppers, then a choice of olives, capers, anchovies or pine nuts. Add garlic and herbs, then cheese if using. Sprinkle with olive oil. Repeat with the remaining dough on a second baking sheet.

Set aside for 30–45 minutes, then bake at 230°C (450°F) Gas 8 for 12–15 minutes or until the bases are blistered and crisp, the toppings aromatic, and the cheeses have melted. Serve hot.

chickpea fritters

Common in Sicily and North Africa, this ancient recipe is a marvellous, easy snack and it can also be served with meat or fish. The ingredients are simple: just chickpea flour, salt, water and parsley.

175 g chickpea flour*

1 teaspoon salt

1 small bunch of flat leaf parsley, chopped

250 ml extra virgin olive oil or olive oil, for frying

a metal tray, about 30 x 40 cm, oiled

Serves 6: makes 24

*Chickpea flour, also known as besan or gram flour, is sold in health food shops, delicatessens and Asian stores.

Sieve the chickpea flour and salt together into a heavy saucepan. Whisk in 500 ml cold water until frothy and lump-free. Bring to the boil, whisking constantly. About 2 minutes after it reaches the boil, it will suddenly thicken – take care or it may splatter. Stir in the parsley.

Keep whisking over the heat for 1 more minute, then pour it out quickly into the oiled tray. Quickly smooth it flat with a spatula to just under 1 cm thickness before it begins to set (about 5–10 minutes).

Mark out into 12 squares, then make diagonal lines to give 24 triangles.

Put the oil in a frying pan or heavy saucepan and heat to 190°C (375°F). Add 6–8 triangles at a time and cook for 2 minutes on each side or until golden, blistered and crisp. Drain on crumpled kitchen paper. Serve hot or warm – they even taste good when cold.

Note The fritters make useful bases for canapés or as 'crisps' to serve with cold, creamy dips. Cut them into tiny rounds or squares and cook as in the main recipe. They can be reheated briefly in a very hot oven for a few minutes before adding any toppings.

A favourite in Egypt, this is almost its national dish.

Ful are dried brown beans, a kind of small broad bean, and look a little like peanuts. I buy mine at Middle Eastern grocers or delis. You can also use canned ful.

ful medames

500 g dried ful medames (dried broad beans) or 1 kg cooked or canned, then drained

2 onions, 1 halved lengthways, 1 halved and finely sliced (reserve the onion skins)

6 very fresh eggs

4 tablespoons extra virgin olive oil

4 garlic cloves, crushed

3–4 teaspoons cumin seeds, coarsely crushed

2–3 teaspoons salt

1 large bunch of fresh flat leaf parsley, mint or coriander

sea salt and freshly ground black pepper

To serve

4–6 tablespoons extra virgin olive oil

2 lemons, cut into wedges or chunks

4 warmed flatbreads

Serves 6–8: makes 1.5 litres

If using dried beans, put them in a large saucepan, cover with 1.25 litres boiling water, cover with a lid and let soak for 2 hours.

Add 2 onion halves, bring to the boil, reduce the heat and simmer, covered, for 2½–3 hours on top of the stove. Alternatively, transfer to a flameproof casserole and cook in a preheated oven at 130°C (250°F) Gas ½ for 6 hours, or until the beans can be easily squashed. Drain and reserve the cooking water.

Wrap the eggs in the reserved onion skins, if using, then put them into some of the hand-hot bean-cooking water. Heat to simmering and cook for 4 minutes. Turn off the heat. Leave for 3 minutes more, rinse, cool, shell and halve.

Heat the olive oil in a frying pan, add the sliced onion, 2–3 teaspoons salt, garlic and cumin seeds and sauté over medium heat until the onions are translucent and aromatic.

Remove from the heat, then add about a third of the cooked beans and 375 ml of the reserved cooking water. Mash them together with a fork or potato masher, then add the remaining beans and half the herbs, chopped. Pour the mixture into a serving dish. Add the egg halves and the remaining herbs. Sprinkle with black pepper and some extra oil, then serve with lemon wedges and warmed flatbreads.

Although butter alone or olive oil and butter together are often used in classic Italian risotto, many chefs maintain that it is the extra olive oil trickled in towards the end that creates real refinement. This risotto uses dried porcini mushrooms, plus fresh wild or field mushrooms. For ease, rice should be measured by volume, not weight.

porcini risotto with fresh and wild mushrooms

15 g dried porcini mushrooms

50 g butter

100 g portobello or other large open mushrooms, quartered, or chanterelles, halved

6 tablespoons extra virgin olive oil

125 ml white wine

250 ml volume Arborio rice

1 onion, sliced

2 garlic cloves, sliced

1 litre boiling chicken or veal stock

8 tablespoons freshly grated Parmesan cheese, about 50 g, plus extra curls, to serve (optional)

sea salt

Serves 4

Put the dried porcini in a small bowl, add 250 ml boiling water and leave for 20 minutes to rehydrate. When plump and aromatic, strain and add the soaking liquid to the hot stock.

Heat the butter in a large heavy saucepan, add the fresh mushrooms and sauté for 5 minutes, turning and stirring now and then. Remove with a slotted spoon and set aside.

Add half the olive oil to the pan, then the rice, onion and garlic. Cook, stirring, for 2 minutes. Add the reserved porcini and wine and cook until absorbed, about 3 minutes. Add 1 ladle (about 250 ml) of hot stock, letting it bubble up, and stirring gently now and then. Continue adding ladles of stock at 5–6 minute intervals or until the rice is tender and the stock has all been used, 22–25 minutes in all – after the last ladle, return the cooked mushrooms to the risotto and add grated Parmesan.

Add salt to taste (cautiously since the grated cheese is also salty). Pour over the reserved 3 tablespoons oil, turn off the heat and serve with extra Parmesan curls on top, if using.

fish, poultry
and meat

Because it is characterful, rich and yet purer than
many other cooking fats, extra virgin works
wonders with seafood, poultry, game and meats
of all kinds. It boosts flavour and aroma,
preserves moisture and succulence and adds
distinction to marinades and bastes. It can be
used to sauté, braise, stew, casserole, bake,
roast, barbecue or grill. Its use will pay dividends
in taste, quality and nutritive value.

Sadly, many people avoid making bouillabaisse at home because the lists of fish and the many processes terrorize them. This is a pity. It is a superb, substantial and glamorous dish for family and friends and can be varied according to the fish available.

bouillabaisse

Heat 2 tablespoons of the olive oil in a very large saucepan. Add the mussels, garlic and wine. Cover the pan and shake over moderate heat for 4–6 minutes or until all the mussels have opened (if any remain closed, discard them).

Tip the pan into a colander lined with wet muslin or kitchen paper set over a bowl to catch the juices. Remove and discard the shells from half the mussels. Set all the mussels aside and return the liquid to the pan. Tie up the parsley and thyme with string and add to the pan. Add the cayenne and stock.

Put a pinch of the saffron into the pan and crush the remainder with 2 teaspoons sea salt using a mortar and pestle. Add a splash of liquid to dissolve the powder, then add it to the pan.

Add the fennel, tomatoes and fish to the pan and return to the boil. Reduce the heat and simmer, part-covered, for 6–8 minutes or until the fish is fairly well cooked. Add the squid and mussels and cover the pan again just long enough to reheat the mussels and cook the squid until firm but not rubbery. Uncover the pan, sprinkle with Pernod, if using, and set aside.

Top the croûtes with rouille and cheese. Put them in deep, heated soup plates, add a share of the fish, seafood and liquid, then serve.

4 tablespoons extra virgin olive oil

750 g mussels, soaked, scrubbed and debearded

4 garlic cloves, crushed

500 ml dry white wine

a pinch of cayenne

1 small bunch of flat leaf parsley

1 small bunch of fresh thyme

1.25 litres fish stock or water

a large pinch of saffron threads

1 head fennel, sliced lengthways

4 large ripe tomatoes, cubed

2 kg assorted prepared white fish, such as cod, snapper, gurnard, mullet, monkfish, bream or conger eel, cut into 5 cm chunks

350 g prepared baby squid, sliced or whole

2 tablespoons Pernod or Ricard, to taste (optional)

sea salt flakes

To serve

croûtes (slices of bread rubbed with garlic and fried in olive oil)

125 ml rouille*, or mayonnaise with harissa (pages 66, 68)

100 g grated Gruyère cheese

kitchen string

Serves 6–8

Sold in jars at good delis.

Treated properly, parsley, garlic and extra virgin olive oil can create a superb, vividly scented green oil that will make any seafood taste good. Trickled over scallops that have been briefly marinated in lemon juice and lovely olive oil, it becomes a sensational recipe altogether.

char-grilled scallops
with parsley oil

2 garlic cloves, crushed

4 tablespoons extra virgin olive oil

juice of 1 lemon

375–400 g plump fresh scallops, about 16

1 small handful of fresh chives (optional), to serve

Parsley oil

1 small bunch of parsley, finely chopped, about 15 g

125 ml extra virgin olive oil

1 garlic clove, crushed

sea salt and freshly ground black pepper

8 short wooden skewers or satay sticks, soaked in water for 30 minutes

Serves 4

Mix the garlic, oil and lemon juice in a shallow, non-metal dish. Pat the scallops dry with kitchen paper. Make shallow criss-cross cuts in each one, 3 times each way on each side. Prick any corals with a cocktail stick to prevent splitting. Add the scallops to the dish of marinade, turn once and set aside while you prepare the parsley oil.

Put the parsley, oil and garlic in a blender and blend until smooth. Strain into a bowl or use straight from the blender.

Drain the scallops, then thread onto the skewers, 2 per skewer. Pour the marinade into a frying pan, bring to the boil and cook until reduced to a sticky golden glaze. Add the scallops and sizzle them in the glaze for 1 minute each side (or a little longer if preferred). Serve with parsley oil poured over and a separate small dish of oil for dipping. Sprinkle with salt and pepper and decorate with a bundle of chives, if using.

Variation If you prefer to barbecue or grill the scallops, put the skewers on an oiled rack 5–6 cm from a very hot barbecue or grill. Sizzle until firm and golden, 3–5 minutes. Put the marinade in a saucepan, bring to the boil and cook until reduced to a sticky glaze.

From Spain and Portugal to the West Indies, bacalau (salt cod) is the classic base for these fishcakes. You can also use smoked cod, smoked haddock or even smoked salmon instead, but if you use the traditional salt cod, it must be softened and desalted – put it in a bowl, cover with cold water and keep in the refrigerator for 24 hours, changing the water every 4 hours.

spanish fishcakes

500 g floury potatoes, halved lengthways

350 ml full-cream milk

350 g smoked haddock or cod, or desalted salt cod

2 tablespoons extra virgin olive oil

1 egg, beaten

4 spring onions, chopped

1 small bunch of fresh coriander, chopped, about 25 g

8 tablespoons plain flour, to coat

6–8 tablespoons virgin olive oil, for frying

sea salt and freshly ground black pepper

lemon or lime wedges, to serve

Serves 4

Cook the potatoes in boiling salted water for 20 minutes. Drain well, return to the still-hot empty saucepan and let dry.

Put the milk in a frying pan, bring to the boil, add the fish and poach gently until flaking and hot, about 6–8 minutes. Drain well, reserving the hot milk. Cool the fish, then skin, bone and flake it.

Add the flaked fish to the saucepan, then the extra virgin olive oil, egg, spring onions, coriander, salt and pepper. Mix and mash to a dense texture, adding ½–1 tablespoon of the hot milk if necessary. Divide the mixture into 8–12 balls. Pat out into flat cakes, then coat in the seasoned flour.

Put most of the olive oil in a non-stick frying pan and heat to 190°C (360°F) or until a 1 cm cube of bread browns in 35–45 seconds. Cook 3–4 fishcakes at a time for 4 minutes on each side. Using a spatula and a slotted spoon, turn them carefully to avoid splashes. Drain on crumpled kitchen paper and keep hot while all the rest are cooked, adding the extra oil to the pan. Serve hot with lime or lemon wedges.

sea bass parcels

A taste of the Mediterranean – fish wrapped in foil and barbecued until tender, served with olive oil flavoured with garlic, capers, lemon juice and anchovies. The result is an intense effect that's not for the faint-hearted!

4 medium whole sea bass or snapper, about 300 g each, or 4 fillets, 150 g each

juice of 1 lemon

125 ml extra virgin olive oil

8 canned anchovy fillets, chopped

2 garlic cloves, chopped

4 tablespoons tiny capers, drained

1 small handful of fresh flat leaf parsley, chopped

sea salt and freshly ground black pepper

4 pieces foil, 25 cm wide, brushed with oil

Serves 4

Make 2 diagonal slashes in both sides of each fish and rub in salt and pepper. Set each fish on a piece of foil. Sprinkle with half the lemon juice. Take the edges of foil parallel to the fish and pinch and roll them together in a tight seal. Loosely pleat or fold the foil lengthways, then pinch and roll the narrow ends until tightly closed.

Cook in a preheated oven at 180°C (350°F) Gas 4 for 10–15 minutes for fillets, or 20–25 minutes for whole fish, or until the flesh is white and firm (open one to test). Alternatively, cook on a barbecue over medium heat for 8–12 minutes for whole fish or 6–8 minutes for fillets.

Meanwhile, using a blender or mortar and pestle, blend the remaining oil with the anchovies, garlic and remaining lemon juice to form a purée. Pour into a bowl, then stir in the capers and parsley. Add extra lemon juice to taste.

Put the fish parcels on 4 heated plates. Open each one just enough to trickle in the sauce, then reseal and serve.

Corn-fed chicken, salty olives and an intense lemon and garlic sauce make this French-style dish distinctive. Choose an olive oil that relates well to the olives and garlic: a lusty, green, fruity, Provençal oil would be perfect. You can also leave the lemon and garlic heads whole and serve a portion to each guest with a spoonful of the juice.

provençal roasted chicken
with garlic, lemons and olives

1.25–1.5 kg free-range, corn-fed chicken, patted dry with kitchen paper

3 tablespoons extra virgin olive oil

2 lemons

1 large bunch of fresh thyme

175 g black olives, such as dry-cured Provençal

4 whole heads of garlic

125 ml full-bodied red wine (optional)

sea salt and freshly ground black pepper

Serves 4

Rub the skin of the chicken with a little olive oil and sprinkle with salt inside and out. Put in a roasting tin breast side down.

Slice the lemons crossways in a series of parallel slashes, but leave them attached at the base. Put half the thyme and one of the lemons inside the cavity and push more thyme between the trussed legs and underneath the bird. Push the olives under the bird. Add the remaining lemon to the tin.

Slice a 'lid' off the top of each garlic head. Pour 1 teaspoon olive oil over each one and replace the lids. Brush the remaining oil over the chicken and lemon.

Roast the chicken breast side down in a preheated oven at 220°C (425°F) Gas 7 for 40 minutes. Turn the bird on its back, put the prepared garlic heads underneath and roast for 35–40 minutes more until deep golden brown. Remove the chicken, garlic and olives from the pan. Let stand, covered, in a warm place for 8–10 minutes until ready to serve.

To make a sauce, mash 3 of the softest garlic cloves into the wine, cooking juices and sediment in the roasting tin, then stir over moderate heat for 3 minutes. Serve with the chicken.

Chicken wings have a natural, sweet stickiness and this can be enhanced by marinating, then cooking over the coals or under a grill. The marinade, boiled down, becomes a rich sauce that is also used to glaze the wings. Olive oil, along with an acid ingredient such as vinegar, wine or tomatoes, softens and tenderizes tougher cuts: a tip to remember for all lean, tougher cuts of poultry, meat and game.

char-grilled chicken wings

12 large chicken wings

Marinade

4 garlic cloves, chopped

2 teaspoons ground ginger

2 tablespoons soy sauce

4 tablespoons balsamic vinegar

1 tablespoon honey

8 tablespoons extra virgin olive oil

125 ml green ginger wine or white wine

To serve

salad leaves

lemon or lime wedges

Serves 6

Twist, then tuck the tips of the chicken wings neatly over the first joint to make a triangle shape. Pierce them all over with a skewer so the marinade can penetrate.

Put the garlic, ginger, soy sauce, vinegar, honey, olive oil and wine in a blender and purée well. Put the wings in a plastic bag and pour in the marinade. Knead and press the marinade all over the wings until well coated, then twist the bag closed. Leave for at least 30 minutes or up to 8 hours.

Heat a barbecue or grill to medium heat. Drain the wings and pour the marinade into a small saucepan. Grill the chicken until dark, sticky and tender, about 12–20 minutes, turning them once (the time may vary, according to the size of the wings).

Bring the marinade to the boil and simmer until it becomes thick and sticky. Brush or spoon over the chicken wings and serve them with a few salad leaves, lemon or lime wedges and a separate bowl of any leftover marinade for dipping. The wings are best eaten with fingers, so provide lots of paper napkins.

Stiphado is the Greek word for a rich casserole. In the past, it was often made from wild rabbit or hare. If it is cooked on top of the stove – the case in many island households in Greece where there is no oven – it becomes a stew. Serve this dish with wide noodles or with plain rice.

turkey stiphado

125 ml extra virgin olive oil, preferably Greek

750 g turkey or chicken breast, cut into 5 cm chunks

2 cinnamon sticks, broken

1 teaspoon allspice berries or cloves, lightly crushed

3–4 sprigs fresh rosemary

125 ml robust red wine

2 tablespoons tomato purée, preferably Greek

1 teaspoon sugar

2 tablespoons red wine vinegar

250 ml chicken or turkey stock

250 g baby onions, peeled, but left whole

250 g Jerusalem artichokes or potatoes, halved lengthways

sea salt and freshly ground black pepper

350 g flat, wide, dried pasta (any type), to serve

Serves 6

Heat half the olive oil in a large flameproof casserole or heavy saucepan and sauté the turkey or chicken pieces until browned on both sides. Add the cinnamon, allspice or cloves, rosemary, red wine, tomato purée, sugar, vinegar and stock. Bring to the boil, reduce the heat, cover and simmer for 25 minutes or until almost done.

Heat the remaining oil in a large frying pan, add the baby onions and artichokes or potatoes and brown them over moderate heat. Transfer to the casserole, stir, cover with a lid and cook for a further 10–15 minutes or until tender.

While the artichokes and onions are cooking, put the pasta in a large pan of boiling salted water, return to the boil and cook, uncovered, for 8–12 minutes or according to the packet instructions, until *al dente*. Drain, then serve with the stiphado.

Variation Toss the pasta in extra olive oil before serving.

The Moroccan spice mix, *ras-el-hanout*, is a blend – it means 'head of the shop' – that is usually made to order. You can get it ready-made in some Middle Eastern stores, which will also sell pickled lemons.

moroccan chicken tagine

2 tablespoons ras-el-hanout or 2 teaspoons mixed spice

½ teaspoon saffron powder

2 teaspoons mild paprika

2 teaspoons sea salt flakes

4 garlic cloves, crushed

6 tablespoons extra virgin olive oil

750 g chicken thighs, skinned

2 pickled lemons, quartered

250 g cooked or canned and drained chickpeas

75 g whole blanched almonds, about 25

2 onions, sliced

2 cinnamon sticks, split lengthways

125–250 ml boiling chicken stock

6 tablespoons honey

65 g seedless raisins

175 g instant couscous

500 ml boiling chicken stock or salted water

Serves 4

Put the ras-el-hanout or mixed spice, saffron, paprika and salt in a small blender and grind to a powder. Alternatively, use a mortar and pestle. Add the garlic and a little of the oil to form a paste.

Pat the chicken dry with kitchen paper, then rub the spice mixture all over until well coated. Remove and discard the flesh from the lemons and slice the peel.

Put a layer of chickpeas, almonds and onions in a heavy saucepan. Add a layer of chicken, then the cinnamon, stock, honey and remaining oil. Add the raisins and sliced lemon peel. Bring to the boil, reduce the heat and simmer for about 45 minutes.

Meanwhile, put the couscous in a heatproof bowl, add the boiling stock or water and set aside to absorb for 5 minutes, stirring at the end. Reheat in the oven or microwave before serving with the tagine.

Lean, best end of prime lamb, effortless to eat, is trimmed of excess chine bone so it can be roasted and sliced into tiny cutlets, 3–4 per person, each with its tiny handle of bone. The ends of the bones should be scraped ('French-trimmed') so they cook cleanly and you can pick them up with your fingers. Ask your butcher to do this if your supermarket doesn't stock this cut.

rack of lamb with roasted baby vegetables

2 racks of lamb, about 300 g each, French-trimmed and chined by the butcher

1 tablespoon cracked black pepper

1 tablespoon balsamic vinegar

1 tablespoon sun-dried tomato paste

125 ml extra virgin olive oil

350 g butternut squash or pumpkin, cut into 1 cm chunks

350 g baby new potatoes, scrubbed well and halved lengthways

4–6 tablespoons red wine

4 sprigs of fresh herbs, such as mint, parsley or rosemary

sea salt

Serves 4

Pat the lamb dry with kitchen paper. Put the pepper in a small bowl, add the vinegar, sun-dried tomato paste and 1 tablespoon of the oil and mix to a purée. Brush or rub the mixture all over the lamb. Chill while you prepare the vegetables.

Put the butternut and potatoes cut side down in a shallow roasting tin. Leave at least a quarter of the area clear for the lamb, which will be added later. Pour the remaining olive oil over the vegetables and sprinkle with about 1 tablespoon crushed sea salt.

Roast towards the top of a preheated oven at 200°C (400°F) Gas 6 for 30 minutes. Add the 2 racks of lamb, side by side, with the bones pointing upwards. Continue roasting for a further 20–25 minutes, until the outside is brown, the inside faintly pink.

Remove the lamb from the oven and let it rest in a warm place for 5–10 minutes to set the juices. Add the red wine to the roasting tin. Heat on top of the stove, stirring frequently, until reduced to a sauce.

Slice the lamb into cutlets, stack 3–4 on each plate with the vegetables, then serve with a spoonful of sauce.

Many Mexican recipes for pork, especially pork loin or tenderloin fillet, use a spicy mix to add flavour, colour and sometimes tenderness. Pork can be sliced and used in whatever way you choose: in salad, on rice, in tortillas, wrapped in leaves or on a purée of sweet potato or pumpkin or with grilled vine tomatoes.

pork with recado

750 g pork loin, cut into 2 cm slices

6 tablespoons extra virgin olive oil

1½ tablespoons fruit or cider vinegar

Recado

1 red onion, cut crossways into 1 cm slices

4 garlic cloves, peeled

1 tablespoon hot red paprika

1 tablespoon annatto powder (optional)

1 teaspoon allspice berries

1 teaspoon black peppercorns

2 teaspoons coarse crystal salt

1 teaspoon dried oregano, pan-toasted

Serves 3–4

Pat the meat dry with kitchen paper. Mix half the olive oil with the fruit vinegar in a cup. Put the meat in a large plastic bag, add the olive oil mixture and toss to coat. Set aside to marinate in the refrigerator for at least 30 minutes or up to 2 hours.

To make the recado, put the onion and garlic on a preheated, non-stick frying pan or stove-top grill pan. Cook dry (without oil) until toasty, dark and soft. Put the onion and garlic in a food processor, then add the paprika, annatto, allspice, peppercorns, salt and oregano and process to a thick paste. Alternatively, use a mortar and pestle.

Pour the marinade out of the plastic bag into a bowl. Add the paste to the bag, then knead and rub to coat all the surfaces.

Preheat a barbecue or grill until very hot. Remove the meat from the bag and barbecue or grill about 5 cm from the heat for 8–10 minutes on each side, then serve hot or cold.

Optional Put the marinade in a saucepan, bring to the boil and reduce to half its volume. Use as a dip, dressing or sauce.

roast pork with crackling

1 teaspoon black peppercorns

1 tablespoon fresh lovage or sage leaves, chopped

2 kg rump end of boneless pork loin, rind scored at 5 mm intervals, patted dry with kitchen paper

2 garlic cloves, crushed

3 tablespoons balsamic vinegar

4 tablespoons extra virgin olive oil

2 large carrots, halved lengthways then crossways

2 onions, skins on, halved crossways

250 ml red wine or cider

sea salt

Serves 8

Using a mortar and pestle, grind 1 tablespoon of the sea salt with the peppercorns and lovage or sage until fine. Rub half the mixture into the scored lines on the pork so none is left on the surface of the rind.

Add the garlic and 1 tablespoon of the balsamic vinegar to the mixture and grind again. Rub the mixture all over the meat, but not on the rind. Rub 2 tablespoons of the olive oil over the rind, then rub in 1 tablespoon sea salt (to help form the crackling).

Mix the remaining oil with the remaining balsamic vinegar, then pour into the roasting tin. Add the pork, rind up, and set aside while you heat the oven to 230°C (450°F) Gas 8.

Roast in the preheated oven for 25 minutes at the highest heat, then reduce to 220°C (425°F) Gas 7. Add the carrots, onions and 250 ml boiling water. Continue cooking for 30 minutes or until a meat thermometer inserted in the centre of the pork registers 75–80°C (170–175°F). Remove the pork from the oven and set aside to rest in a warm place, uncovered.

Discard the most frizzled, dark portions of carrot and onion but chop about 125 ml of the thickest parts into a blender. Stir the wine or cider into the roasting tin and bring to the boil, stirring to dissolve all the sticky sediment. Cook for several minutes more, then pour it all into the blender.

Blend for 1–2 minutes to form a thick purée-like sauce. Pour it back into the roasting tin and reheat, adding extra water if it is too thick, or boiling it down if it is too thin. Carve the pork into thick, chunky slices and serve with the sauce.

This elegant dish combines rich and fascinating flavours – beef, truffle oil, thyme, garlic, full-flavoured flat mushrooms. The sliced rare beef is set on a fresh salad and Parmesan curls are added as seasoning.

char-grilled beef fillet
with field mushrooms

4 filet mignons, 250 g each, well aged, at room temperature

Marinade

6 tablespoons estate-bottled, first-pressed, extra virgin olive oil

2 tablespoons truffle oil

1 tablespoon sherry vinegar

1 teaspoon black peppercorns, coarsely crushed

1 small bunch of fresh thyme sprigs

4 large open mushrooms

2 garlic cloves, crushed

1 teaspoon sea salt

Salad

2 handfuls of rocket leaves

2 handfuls of watercress

2 handfuls lamb's lettuce

100 g radishes, sliced crossways

100 g Parmesan cheese, cut into long shavings with a vegetable peeler

Serves 4

Pat the beef dry with kitchen paper. Put it in a plastic bag, add 3 tablespoons of the olive oil, the truffle oil, vinegar, peppercorns and thyme. Knead gently together. Seal the bag loosely and marinate in the refrigerator for 30 minutes.

Heat a barbecue or stove-top grill pan to moderate. To make the salad, put the rocket, watercress, lamb's lettuce, radishes and Parmesan in a bowl, toss gently, then pile onto 4 serving plates. Trickle with the remaining olive oil.

Remove the beef from the bag, drain, then add to the barbecue or grill pan. Put the mushrooms in the plastic bag, add the garlic and sea salt and knead until the marinade has been evenly absorbed.

Cook the beef fillets for 5–6 minutes on each side or until well marked in lines, aromatic and dark, but still pink inside. Transfer to a heated plate and let stand, covered.

Cook the mushrooms for 2–3 minutes on each side or until dark and toasty. Cut in halves or quarters.

Slice each fillet crossways into 5–6 slices and set on top of the salad. Add the mushrooms, then serve.

Elizabeth David's Provençal daube was the first of its type I ever tasted – rich with red wine, baby onions and orange zest. My version contains walnut halves and Cognac – heart-warming, welcoming and grand. Use greeny-gold extra virgin olive oil, the best you've got.

boeuf en daube

4 tablespoons extra virgin olive oil

4 garlic cloves, sliced

125 g thick-cut unsmoked bacon or bacon lardons, cubed

3 carrots, halved lengthways

12–16 baby onions, peeled

1 kg beef, such as shoulder or topside, cut into 1 cm thick slices, then into 6 cm squares

6 plum tomatoes, skinned, then thickly sliced

zest of 1 orange, removed in one piece

1 bunch of fresh herbs, such as parsley, thyme, bay leaf and rosemary, tied with kitchen string

60 g walnut halves

250 ml robust red wine

2 tablespoons Cognac or brandy

150 ml beef stock or water

sea salt

chopped flat leaf parsley, to serve

Serves 4–6

Heat the oil in a large flameproof casserole and sauté the garlic, bacon, carrots and onions for 4–5 minutes or until aromatic. Remove from the casserole. Put a layer of meat in the bottom of the casserole, then add half the sautéed vegetable mixture and a second layer of meat. Add the remaining vegetable mixture, the tomatoes, orange zest, bundle of herbs and walnuts.

Put the wine in a small saucepan and bring to the boil. Add the Cognac or brandy and warm for a few seconds, shaking the pan a little, to let the alcohol cook away. Pour the hot liquids over the meat with just enough stock so that it's barely covered.

Heat the casserole until simmering, then cover with foil and a lid and simmer gently for 2 hours or until the meat is fork tender and the juices rich and sticky.

The dish can also be cooked in the oven. Just bring to the boil over high heat, reduce to simmering, cover with foil, replace the lid and cook in the oven at 150°C (300°F) Gas 2 for 2½ hours or until very tender.

Sprinkle with parsley and serve hot either absolutely plain, or with pasta, mashed potatoes or rice.

breads and
sweet things

Extra virgin adds great allure to many sweet doughs, batters and even pastries, if the proportions are appropriate and the techniques adapted to suit. These foods become healthier because of the reduction in saturated fats, but browning, richness, crispness and tenderness may all benefit as well.

focaccia with olives

1 sachet easy-blend dried yeast (7 g)

250 g plain white flour, plus 4 tablespoons for shaping

½ teaspoon sea salt flakes

2 tablespoons extra virgin olive oil, preferably Italian

Topping

finely shredded zest of 2 oranges and the juice of 1

4 tablespoons extra virgin olive oil

2 garlic cloves, crushed

2 tablespoons fresh rosemary leaves, coarsely chopped

½ teaspoon coarsely crushed black pepper

1 teaspoon sea salt flakes or crystals

150 g dry-cured black olives

Serves 4

I developed this quick food processor dough for pizzas, but it makes excellent focaccia too. Olive oil is used in both the rich, flavourful topping and the dough itself – it is delicious as well as authentic and eminently practical, since there is no need to rub the flour into the fat or oil.

Put the yeast, flour and sea salt in a food processor fitted with a plastic blade. Pulse briefly to sift. Mix the oil and 180 ml warm water together and, with the machine running, pour in all at once through the feed tube. Process, in short bursts, for 15 seconds until a soft mass forms (not a ball). It will be sticky and soft.

Scoop out the dough adding the extra 4 tablespoons flour as you knead, roll, pat and thump down the dough for 2 minutes. Put the ball of dough in an oiled bowl. Enclose the whole bowl in a large plastic bag. Leave in a warm place until the dough has doubled in size, about 50 minutes.

Pat and stretch the dough into a rectangle about 32 x 22 cm. Transfer to an oiled oven tray. Prod the dough all over with your fingertips to form dimples to take the topping.

Mix the orange zest and juice, oil, garlic, rosemary, pepper and half the salt in a bowl. Pour the mixture over the dough. Scatter with the olives, pushing them well into the dimples. Set aside for 30 minutes to rest the dough.

Bake in a pre-heated oven at 200°C (400°F) Gas 6 for 25–30 minutes or until crusty and aromatic. Sprinkle with the remaining salt. Cut into generous squares, then serve hot or warm, with a glass of fruity red wine.

Make these doughnuts some cool or wintry morning, close your eyes and dream of Barcelona. It is essential to cook the churros batter in very hot olive oil, so the outside crisps and seals quickly and the batter inside is cooked by steam. Dip the churros into hot chocolate before eating.

churros with hot chocolate

350 g self-raising flour

½ teaspoon salt

1 egg, beaten

400–450 ml milk

olive oil, for frying

To coat

8 tablespoons caster sugar

4 tablespoons powdered cinnamon (optional)

Hot chocolate

250 g bitter dark chocolate, chopped or grated

600 ml milk, boiled

a piping bag with a 1–2 cm plain nozzle

Serves 4

Sieve the flour and salt into a bowl. Make a hollow in the centre. Whisk the egg in a bowl with 250 ml of the milk. Pour into the hollow and mix into the flour. Gradually whisk in enough of the remaining milk to make a smooth, creamy, thick batter able to be piped easily. Transfer to a piping bag with plain nozzle.

Pour 10 cm depth of olive oil into a heavy saucepan fitted with a frying basket. Heat it to 190°C (375°F) or until a cube of bread browns in 35 seconds.

Pipe long, spiralled, coiled-up lengths directly into the oil. Let sizzle and cook for 4–6 minutes or until golden and spongy, not raw, in the centre (test one to check).

Lift the churros out of the oil using the basket or tongs. Drain on crumpled kitchen paper. Repeat using the remaining batter.

When cool, scissor-snip the churros into 15 cm lengths. Put the sugar in a shallow plate, mix in the cinnamon, if using, then roll the pieces in the mixture.

To make the hot chocolate, whisk the chocolate and boiled milk in a small saucepan, whisking and cooking until well blended and dusky brown. Serve with the churros.

This Mediterranean cake takes me back to Sicily with its hillsides of olive, orange and lemon trees, almonds in baskets and bottles of orange flower water – redolent of its Arab past. Instead of flour there is semolina and ground almonds. Instead of butter, there is oil and no dairy products whatsoever.

semolina citrus cake

shredded or grated zest and juice of 1 lemon

shredded or grated zest and juice of 1 orange

185 ml extra virgin olive oil

215 g caster sugar

¼ teaspoon salt

3 medium eggs

200 g semolina

115 g ground almonds

1 teaspoon baking powder

1 teaspoon almond essence

1 teaspoon orange flower water

4 tablespoons Cointreau, Grand Marnier or limoncello

a loose-based round cake tin, 23 cm in diameter, lightly oiled and base-lined

Serves 8–12

Reserve a little of the shredded lemon and orange zest and put the remainder in a bowl with the oil, sugar, salt, orange and lemon juice and eggs. Whisk with an electric or balloon whisk until well mixed and smooth.

Sieve the semolina and baking powder into a second bowl and add the ground almonds. Fold the almond essence and orange flower water into the egg mixture. Pour all at once into the dry ingredients, fold together, but do not overmix. Spoon into the prepared tin and smooth the top.

Bake towards the top of a preheated oven at 160°C (325°F) Gas 3 for 40–45 minutes or until pale gold at the edges and firm in the middle. A skewer pushed into the centre should come out clean.

Remove from the oven and let it cool in the tin for about 10 minutes. Trickle the liqueur over the top. Push the cake out, still on its loose metal base, and let cool on a wire rack for another 10 minutes. Remove the base and paper. Serve in 8–12 wedges, warm or cool, but not chilled.

The cake will keep in an airtight container for up to 4 days.

There is a general belief in Greece that walnuts or almonds and honey will increase the bridegroom's prowess in the bedroom. No wonder, since Greek honey is absolutely outstanding.

greek honey, walnut and brandy cake

125 ml extra virgin olive oil

100 g caster sugar

2 medium eggs

200 g walnut pieces

185 g self-raising flour, sieved

¼ teaspoon salt

125 ml strained plain Greek yoghurt or thick-set yoghurt

2 tablespoons brandy, preferably Greek Metaxa

2 tablespoons clear honey

a loose-based round cake tin, 20 cm in diameter, oiled and base-lined

Serves 8–12

Put the oil, sugar and eggs in a large bowl and whisk with an electric beater until smooth. Reserve a handful of the walnuts for decoration and chop the remainder with a knife or food processor in brief bursts until fine, but not mealy.

Add to the bowl, then add the flour, salt and yoghurt. Using broad strokes, mix the batter with a wooden spoon until smooth and even. Do not overmix.

Spoon the mixture into the prepared cake tin and smooth flat on top. Scatter with the reserved nuts.

Bake towards the top of a preheated oven at 175°C (340°F) Gas 3½ for 40 minutes. Test the centre – a skewer inserted at an angle into the centre should come out clean.

Mix the brandy and honey in a small bowl, then trickle the mixture over the cake. Let it cool in the tin for 20 minutes.

Remove the cake, still on its loose metal base, and cool on a wire rack for 10 minutes. Remove the base, peel off the paper and serve warm or cold.

index

Author's acknowledgements

In **Britain**, my thanks go to my patient researcher Robert Larkins, Christine Boodle, Barrabel and Katie Mason, María José Sevilla (Spanish Embassy Commercial Office), Carmen Veiras (Foods from Spain), Luis Avides (Portuguese Trade Office), A. Kouroussis (Greek Embassy), Sevda Ramadan (Turkish Embassy), Nabil Ben Khedhar (Tunisian Embassy), The Italian Trade Centre, C.R. Kaid (Embassy of Algeria), Daphna Sternfeld (Embassy of Israel), Marianne Malonne (SOPEXA), Charles Carey (The Oil Merchant) and Suzanne Hesketh (Hill & Knowlton). In **Spain**, to Fausto Luchetti, Josep Rocamara and Carlos Mora of Agroles and Asoliva and William Devin of Unió Cooperativa, SCCL. In **France**, thanks to Bryce Attwell, Annik Lesenfant and to Madame F. Person, Ministry of Agriculture. In **New Zealand**, thanks to Jack Hobbs of Albany Olive Press and Gilly and Alastair Chater. In **Australia** to Olives Australia in Queensland. In **California**, to Patty Darragh of the California Olive Oil Council and Michael Coon of the McEvoy Ranch.

Picture credits

Photography by Peter Cassidy (except for the following)
Key: a=above, b=below, r=right, l=left, c=centre
Martin Brigdale: *5, 8l, 8br, 10-11, 12l inset, 24, 26*
Alan Williams: *7, 8ar, 18, 21l, 28c, 30*